Jann Huizenga

TOTALLY TRUE

Building Vocabulary Through Reading

OXFORD

UNIVERSITY PRESS

OXFORD
UNIVERSITY PRESS

198 Madison Avenue
New York, NY 10016 USA

Great Clarendon Street, Oxford OX2 6DP UK

Oxford University Press is a department of the University of Oxford.
It furthers the University's objective of excellence in research, scholarship,
and education by publishing worldwide in

Oxford New York

Auckland Cape Town Dar es Salaam Hong Kong Karachi
Kuala Lumpur Madrid Melbourne Mexico City Nairobi
New Delhi Shanghai Taipei Toronto

With offices in

Argentina Austria Brazil Chile Czech Republic France Greece
Guatemala Hungary Italy Japan Poland Portugal Singapore
South Korea Switzerland Thailand Turkey Ukraine Vietnam

OXFORD and OXFORD ENGLISH are registered trademarks of
Oxford University Press.

© Oxford University Press 2005
Database right Oxford University Press (maker)

Library of Congress Cataloging-in-Publication Data

Huizenga, Jann.
    Totally true : building vocabulary through reading/Jann Huizenga.
        v. cm.
    Includes indexes.
    ISBN : 978-0-19-430203-6 (bk. 1 : student book)
    ISBN : 978-0-19-430206-7 (bk. 1 : class CD)
    [etc.]
    1. Vocabulary—Problems, exercises, etc. 2. English language—
Textbooks for foreign speakers. I. Huizenga, Linda. II. Title.
    PE1449.H83 2005
    428.2'4-dc22

                                            2004059973

Executive Publisher: Nancy Leonhardt
Senior Acquisitions Editor: Chris Balderston
Editor: Emma Gonin
Assistant Editor: Hannah Ryu
Assistant Editor: Kate Schubert
Art Director: Maj-Britt Hagsted
Design Project Manager: Amelia Carling
Designer: Vanessa Bender
Layout Artist: Julie Macus
Senior Art Editor: Jodi Waxman
Art Editor: Justine Eun
Production Manager: Shanta Persaud
Production Controller: Eve Wong

ISBN : 978 0 19 430203 6

Printed in China.

10 9 8 7 6

This book is printed on paper from certified and well- managed sources.

ACKNOWLEDGMENTS

Cover photographs: Sunset: © Fogstock/Alamy; Skydiver: © Buzz Pictures/Alamy;
Surfer: © Buzz Pictures/Alamy; Taipei 101: © Associated Press

Illustrations by: Adrian Barclay pp.4, 7, 19, 31, 47, 59, 71, 76, 82(Beach); Jun Park
pp.12, 16, 24, 26, 72(Match the words), 48, 54(Match the words), 68, 80; George
Thompson pp.15, 26(Girl drawing), 35, 40, 51, 63, 75; Joe VanDerBos pp.8, 20, 36,
44, 52, 60, 64, 82(Match the words);William Waitzman pp.3, 11, 23, 32, 39, 43,
54(kitchen), 67, 79.

We would like to thank the following for their permission to reproduce photographs:
Suzy Allman/New York Times p.58; AP/Wide World Photo p.18; wendy
connett/Alamy p.42; Bill Bachmann/Alamy p.73; Leland Bobbe/Photographer's
Choice/Getty Images p.50; Andrea Brambilla/Spin 360 p.37; Chris Brandis p.70;
Jim Bourg/Reuters/Corbis p.9; Brian Cassey/AP Wide World Photos p.41; Stewart
Charles Cohen/Digital Vision/Getty Images p.22; Comstock Images/Alamy p.25;
Ghislain & Marie David de Lossy/ The Image Bank/Getty Images p.5; Michael
Dunning/Photographer's Choice/Getty Images p.53; Dynamic Graphics
Group/Creatas/Alamy p.61; Alain Evrard/Robert Harding World Imagery/Getty
Images p.17; First Light/ImageState p. 28; Drew Gardner/Guinness World Records
2002 p.74; Scott Ginsberg p.2; David Howells p.49; Jann Huizenga p.30; Sakchai
Lalit/AP Wide World Photos p.38; Mark Lipson/Stone/Getty Images p.56; John
Lok/The Seattle Times p.33; Rick John Molloy/Stone/Getty Images p.46; Brian
Mullennix/Alamy p.65; PictureNet/CORBIS p.45; Pixland/Indexstock p.77; Gary
Porter/The Journal Sentinal p.69; Bill Pugliano/Getty Images p.14; REUTERS/Dan
Chung p.62; REUTERS/Nir Elias p.81; REUTERS/David Loh p.78; REUTERS/Chor
Sokunthea p.6; REUTERS/Shannon Stapleton p.66; RubberBall/Alamy p.84; Toyota
Motor Corporation p.13; Peter Turnley/CORBIS p.21; U.Grill p.34; Zhejiang Geely
Holdings Company p.10.

Special thanks to: Stephanie Luo; MTV Networks International; Nathan's Famous,
Inc.; Toyota Motor Company; Zhejiang Geely Holdings Company.

Unit Tests (available online) written by: Andy London.

Contents

To the Student

Welcome to _Totally True_. Let's take a look at a unit.

1. **Read the story** asks you to predict what the story is about, read it, and get to know the New Words.

2. **Rate the story** asks about your interest in the story.

3. **Check your comprehension** asks how well you understand the story.

4. **Check your vocabulary** helps you practice the New Words by completing sentences about the story.

5. **Listen to the story** gives you the chance to hear the story as you look at the pictures.

6. **Retell the story** helps you practice retelling the story using the pictures.

1

Hello, My Name Is Scott

1. Read the story
Look at the pictures on these pages. What is the story about? Now read it.

ST. LOUIS, USA ¹One day, Scott Ginsberg, 23, went to a meeting* and put on a nametag**. It said, "Hello, my name is Scott." ²After the meeting, Scott forgot all about his nametag and went out to a restaurant with the nametag still on his shirt. ³Strangers were friendly to him and began conversations. "Hello, Scott!" they said. "What's up?***" Scott met 20 people that night and had a wonderful time.

⁴Now Scott wears a nametag all the time—at work and on weekends. ⁵He meets new people everywhere—at parks, movies, and supermarkets. ⁶"Most people want to be friendly," he says. "But they're afraid. Nametags make people comfortable. They break the silence, the walls between people."

*meeting: when two or more people meet to talk
**nametag: a paper with your name that you put on a shirt or coat
***What's up?: What's new?

NEW WORDS

go out _v_	stranger _n_	everywhere _adv_	comfortable _adj_
restaurant _n_	friendly _adj_	park _n_	silence _n_
still _adv_	conversation _n_	make _v_	wall _n_

>> See Glossary on page 88. >>

2. Rate the story
How much did you like it? Mark an ✗.

Not at All   A Lot
1 2 3 4 5

2   Unit 1

3. Check your comprehension
Put the sentences in the correct order. Number them 1–6. The first one is done for you.

a. ___ He now wears a nametag everywhere.
b. ___ Later, he went out to eat with the nametag still on.
c. ___ He had a wonderful time that night!
d. ___ He put on a nametag.
e. _1_ Scott Ginsberg went to a meeting.
f. ___ A lot of strangers talked to Scott.

4. Check your vocabulary
Complete the sentences with the New Words.

a. Scott forgot about his nametag and w_ _ _ out to a rest_ _ _ _ _ _.
b. St_ _ _ _ _ _s began _ _ _ _ersations with him.
c. Nametags, Scott says, m_ _ _ people com_ _ _ _ _ _ _ _.
d. Nametags break the sil_ _ _ _, the w_ _ _s between people.

5. Listen to the story track 2
Now listen to the story two or three times. Look at the pictures below as you listen.

6. Retell the story
Cover the story and look at the pictures above. Retell the story using the New Words.

Unit 1   3

iv

7. Answer the questions asks you to talk about the story and yourself.

8. Learn word partnerships builds on what you have learned by introducing words that go with one or two of the New Words.

9. Learn word groups builds on what you have learned by using pictures to introduce more vocabulary related to the New Words.

---

7. **Answer the questions**

About the story…
a. What happened the first time Scott went out with his nametag on?
b. Where does Scott meet people now?
c. What does Scott say about nametags? What do they do?
d. What do you think? Are people afraid to be friendly?

About you…
e. Do you like to go out on weekends? Where?
f. Where do you meet new people?
g. How do you begin conversations with them?
h. How can we be more friendly?

8. **Learn word partnerships**

Study the partnerships below. Complete the sentences so they are true for you.

GO OUT			
go out	to	a restaurant	***Scott went out to a restaurant.***
		a movie	*On weekends, Young-hee likes to go out to a movie.*
		eat	*I don't often go out to eat at Burger Boy.*
	for	coffee	*My friends love to go out for coffee.*
		dinner	*I went out for dinner yesterday with Ichiro.*

a. My friends and I like to go out _____
b. I don't often _____ out _____
c. I went _____ for _____ with _____

9. **Learn word groups**

Complete the sentences so they are true for you. Use words from the picture.

PLACES TO MEET FRIENDS

a. I like to meet my friends at _____
b. We never meet at _____
c. It's expensive to go out to _____ in my town.

4   Unit 1

---

10. Take a dictation gives you practice listening to a summary of the story and writing down what you hear.

11. Complete the story gives you a second story to review the New Words and other new vocabulary.

Talk about the stories gives you the chance to talk more about both stories.

---

10. **Take a dictation**   track 3
Use your own paper to write the dictation. Check your answers on page 86.

11. **Complete the story**
Use the words from the box to complete the story.

everywhere	strangers	silence	make	parks	friendly

Say Hello!

ROTTERDAM, THE NETHERLANDS   A Dutch politician* did not like the **(1)** _____ in Rotterdam. He wanted to **(2)** _____ people more **(3)** _____. So he put up a big sign** in Rotterdam. "Say Hello," the sign says.

The politician, Joel van der Meer, moved to Rotterdam last year. Before that, he lived in a small town in the north of the Netherlands. There, he says, people say hello to **(4)** _____ on the street, in cafes, and in **(5)** _____. "When I came to Rotterdam last year, I was shocked***. People here don't say hello on the street."

Van der Meer now wants to put up "Say Hello" signs **(6)** _____ in Rotterdam. "I want people to be friends," he says.

* politician: someone who works in the government
** sign: a thing with writing or a picture on it that tells you something
*** shocked: very surprised

 Talk about the stories
How are the stories of Scott Ginsberg and Joel van der Meer similar? How are they different?

Unit 1   5

---

v

Dear Teachers,

Welcome to *Totally True*! If you are looking for an enjoyable and motivating way to help build your students' vocabulary, you've come to the right place. Vocabulary learning doesn't have to be difficult and dull. The goal of *Totally True* Book 1 is to make it fun. It teaches common words in the context of amazing true stories at a beginner level. The book is intended for classroom use, but it will also work well for self-study with the audio CD.

Totally True was written with two things in mind: 1) that everyone loves a great story and 2) that students acquire new vocabulary more readily when they meet it in engaging contexts and then use it in purposeful follow-up activities. Research on vocabulary acquisition shows that most learning takes place when students meet new words in context, not in isolation. The content must be rich and interesting, and—even more importantly—understandable. The stories in *Totally True* satisfy these conditions: they are intrinsically entertaining while the accompanying pictures make them easy to understand.

The research suggests that context alone, however, is not enough for many students to learn new vocabulary. Formal, explicit instruction can help. Thus *Totally True* highlights new vocabulary in the opening stories and helps students to focus on this vocabulary in varied activities throughout the rest of each unit. How can we make sure that new vocabulary will remain in students' long-term memories? At least two things are necessary: First, students need to process the vocabulary at a deep level—that is, they need to produce it. *Totally True* provides many opportunities for students to use the new vocabulary items in both speaking and writing, in meaningful and personalized ways. Second, students need multiple meaningful exposures to the vocabulary (as many as 7–12 times, some experts say). *Totally True* provides careful recycling—students revisit each new vocabulary item several times within each unit, as well as in the review units, and to some extent from unit to unit. The index on pages 97–99 shows where the vocabulary items are recycled. *Totally True* thoroughly integrates the four strands of listening, reading, speaking, and writing, and its activities are sequenced so that work on receptive skills precedes production. The book can be successfully used for general language acquisition or reading instruction as well as for the specific mastery of vocabulary.

I encourage you to adapt the material to suit the needs of your classes. I really hope you enjoy using the book, and I wish you every success.

Jann Huizenga

Totally *Bookworms* Compatible

A key benefit of *Totally True* is that its language levels are tied to the *Oxford Bookworms* syllabus, so the series can be used together with *Bookworms* graded readers. The stories in *Totally True* Book 1 use the core structures and the vocabulary from *Bookworms* Stage 1. However, each opening story introduces 11–14 words above Stage 1. These words are highlighted in the story and treated as "New Words." Meeting these higher-level New Words initially in the rich context of

a story helps students to understand them. Students continue to meet and produce the New Words in the activities throughout the unit, ensuring that these words become part of students' active vocabulary. Studying with *Totally True* Book 1 will help prepare students to move up to *Bookworms* Stage 2. *Totally True* can also complement any other extensive reading program. The stories and carefully designed practice activities will provide variety in teaching reading.

Level	Vocabulary	Core structures include:	Examples from *Totally True*
Oxford Bookworms Stage 1 and *Totally True* Book 1	400 headwords	simple present present continuous simple past	The boy does not like to be away from his **favorite** friend. Once the family took a trip, but they did not stay away long. "My son **missed** Lucky," said his mother. "So we came back early." *Python Boy* (Unit 2)
Oxford Bookworms Stage 2 and *Totally True* Book 2	700 headwords	present perfect *will* (future) *have to / must not could*	The city has given free books to subway riders **since** 2004, and wants to **give away** millions more in the future. The city hopes that readers will **return** the books when they finish, but no one is checking. *Fighting Crime with Books* (Unit 13)
Oxford Bookworms Stage 3 and *Totally True* Book 3	1,000 headwords	present perfect continuous past perfect *used to*	**Meanwhile**, their dinner was still cooking on the **stove** in the kitchen. They had completely forgotten about it! It started to burn, and the **flames** jumped quickly around the kitchen. The whole room and a nearby hallway were completely destroyed. *Cat and Couple Are Homeless* (Unit 13)

1. Read the story

Purpose: To engage students' attention, to train them to use prediction as a pre-reading strategy, to develop general reading comprehension skills, and to introduce the New Words in context.

Procedure: Before students read, ask them to cover the story and look at the pictures on the opposite page. As students make predictions about the story, help them with the vocabulary they need—especially key words and New Words from the story. If students call out words or phrases in their native language, translate them into English and write them on the board. Then ask students to read the story silently to see if their predictions are correct. Tell them to make their best guess about the meanings of the New Words—the words in bold. Tell students the numbered sentences in the story correspond to the numbered pictures. Within the context of the story and with the support of the pictures, students should be able to make good guesses.

After the first reading, students can check the meanings of the New Words in the glossary on pages 88–96. As many of the New Words are irregular verbs, there is an irregular verb list on page 100 in Totally True Book 1. This means students at this level can easily check the simple past and the past participle of these verbs. Encourage them to read the story again after this.

Alternative procedure: After students look at the pictures, ask them to write two or three questions they have about the story. Ask them to read the story to see if they can find answers to their questions.

2. Rate the story

Purpose: To encourage students to respond personally to the story and to develop critical reading and thinking skills, such as evaluating and giving opinions.

Procedure: After students mark an ✗ on the scale, ask them to share the reasons for their ratings with a partner or a small group.

Instead of having students do the "Rate the story" activity here, you could have them do it after activity 7. Alternatively, they could rate the story here and again

after activity 7 to see if their opinions have changed.

Alternative procedure: If you have a small class, hang five pieces of paper in different places on the wall of your classroom. Each paper shows a different number from 1 to 5. After students have marked an ✗ on the scale, ask them to stand up and walk to the number that shows how they rated the story. Ask them to speak to one member of their group to explain their opinion of the story. After a minute, ask a few volunteers to share what they heard with the whole class.

3. Check your comprehension

Purpose: To see how well students understand the general meaning of the story.

Procedure: Encourage students to complete this activity without looking back at the story. Then have students compare their answers with a partner or a small group. If the activity causes difficulty, have students read the story a second time and try the activity again.

4. Check your vocabulary

Purpose: To help students focus on the use and spelling of the New Words, a first step in making the New Words part of their active vocabulary.

Procedure: Encourage students to complete this activity without looking back at the story. Then have students check their answers against the story or compare them with a partner or small group.

Alternative procedure: If the activity causes difficulty, have students complete it while looking at the story.

5. Listen to the story

Purpose: To give students an opportunity to hear the story and the New Words, and to prepare them to retell the story.

Procedure: Ask students to look only at the numbered pictures (not at the story). Play the CD. Students will probably want to hear the story more than once. Afterward, to assess students' listening, read the story to students yourself, making some factual "mistakes." Tell students to clap when they hear a mistake and

then see if anyone in the class can correct it.
If you don't have the CD, read the story to students yourself. Say the numbers as you read so that students can look at the relevant picture at the right time.
Alternative procedure: To reinforce the New Words, write them on the board and point to them as the CD is playing. This will be especially appreciated by your more visually-oriented students.

6. Retell the story

Purpose: To give students oral practice, with a combined focus on story retelling and additional practice of the New Words.

Procedure: Have students cover the story and look only at the pictures. Elicit the story orally from the whole class first. Encourage students to call out the ideas of the story in chronological order and to use the New Words, telling them to paraphrase. Then ask students to practice retelling the story in their own words with a partner.

Alternative procedure: Put students in small groups and have them retell the entire story together by taking turns contributing a sentence at a time.

7. Answer the questions

Purpose: To encourage students to discuss the story, to relate it to their personal lives, and to meet and use the New Words in meaningful and personalized contexts.

Procedure: Ask students one of the questions from this activity. Give them time to think about the answer and then have them discuss it with a partner or a small group. Ask a volunteer or two to report back to the whole class. Then ask another question.

Alternative procedure for "About the story":
To make sure all your students are involved in this activity simultaneously, follow this procedure:

  a. Put students in small groups. Four is the ideal number.
  b. Give each student a number (from 1 to 4).
  c. Ask one of the "About the story" questions.

  d. Tell students to decide on the answer together in their groups.
  e. After about a minute, call a number (1, 2, 3, or 4). Have students with that number stand up and report back on their group's answer.

Alternative procedure for "About you": To provide students with some writing practice, allow each student to choose the one question that most interests him/her. Give students a time limit of about five minutes to write their answers. Then have students share their answers with a small group.

8. Learn word partnerships

Purpose: To build on what students have learned by introducing key collocations for one or two of the New Words.

Procedure: Tell students that they are going to learn a little more about one or two of the New Words. Have students study the chart. Explain that the New Word(s) in black often occur(s) with the words in blue. Tell students that when they meet any new vocabulary, they should look at the words that surround it because learning a new word together with its "word partners" will lead to fluency faster than learning a word in isolation. This technique will also make them more accurate users of the language. Have students complete the sentences individually, and then ask them to share their answers with a partner or a small group.

9. Learn word groups

Purpose: To build on what students have learned by introducing new vocabulary that is thematically related to one or more of the New Words.

Procedure: Students already know one or two of the New Words pictured here, but they may not know the other words that are thematically related to it/them. Pronounce the words and allow students to repeat them. Then have students complete the sentences and share their answers with a partner or a small group.

10. Take a dictation

Purpose: To assess if students can hear and write the New Words in a story summary.

Procedure: Play the dictation on the CD and ask students to write what they hear—there is a pause after each breath group so they have time to write. Play the dictation again to allow students to check their answers. Students then correct their work or their partner's work by looking at pages 86–87. You could use this as a test and collect the dictations.

Alternative procedure: Read the dictation yourself at normal speed. Students should not write at this stage. Then read it again, pausing after each breath group so that students have time to write. Read the dictation a third time, at near-normal speed, allowing students to check their answers. Students then correct their work or their partner's work by looking at pages 86–87. Again, you could use this as a test and collect the dictations.

11. Complete the story

Purpose: To give students an opportunity to review the New Words, and other vocabulary from the unit, in a new context, and to provide additional reading practice using a story that is thematically related to the first one.

Procedure: Encourage students to complete this story individually, and then have them check their answers with a partner or a small group. They could then practice reading the story to each other.

Alternative procedure: If you have more advanced students, have them cover the story and try to retell it in their own words, using the words in the box.

Talk about the stories

Purpose: To give students additional oral practice using the New Words in a less structured way, and to develop critical thinking skills such as evaluating, comparing, contrasting, and giving opinions.

Procedure: There are two types of "Talk about the stories": discussion questions and role plays. For the discussion questions, give students a bit of thinking time. Then have them discuss their ideas with a small group or you could conduct a whole-class discussion.

For the role plays, have students work with a partner. Give them a time limit of a few minutes for their "conversation." You may have brave volunteers who want to reenact their conversation for the whole class!

Web Searches

If your students want additional information about a story, have them do a Web search by inserting a name or a topic into a search engine. This could be done as classwork or homework. At the time of publication, most of the stories could be found on the Internet.

Audio CD

The CD contains recordings of the first stories in each unit and the dictations. These are read by native speakers and provide great listening models and variety in class. You may prefer to play the story for students in activity 1, changing the focus of the activity from reading comprehension to pronunciation.

Totally True Teacher's Resource Site

The Teacher's Resource Site has downloadable Unit Tests that review all the New Words from each unit and help teachers and students assess progress. Answer Keys for these tests and for *Totally True* Book 1 are also available at www.oup.com/elt/teacher/totallytrue.

Acknowledgments

I would like to thank those folks who helped me find the great stories for this book—my generous and talented colleagues Won-Mi Jeong and Stella Chen, my brother Joel (with his piles of clippings), and my stalwart husband Kim (who spent countless hours finding and critiquing stories and then figuring out how to illustrate them). Thanks also to my father, John, who never complained when his tidy kitchen was transformed into my temporary office during visits.

I am also grateful to all the teachers and students in Asia who have participated in my recent workshops. Their creative ideas and enthusiasm helped shape this series. These people include the brilliant and hospitable teachers and students at De Lin Institute of Technology in Taipei—in particular Fanny Lai, Stella Chen, Felisa Li, Gloria Chen, and Shi-tung Chuang; the unforgettable teachers from the Korean National University of Education—especially Won-Mi Jeong, Eun-Jeong Ji, Young-Chai Son, Hee-Jung Park, Sun-Mi Kim, Jin-a Choe, Young-Hee Moon, Hyo-Gyoung Lim, and Joo-In Chang; and all the dear colleagues from Kumamoto Prefecture in Japan—including Rika Muraoka, Naomi Osada, Masaya Shindate, Hideaki Kiya, and Yayoi Umeda. It was an honor to work with everyone.

I'd like to give a special, heartfelt thanks to Dorota Holownia and Candy Veas, whose creativity and high spirits, as well as their intellectual and moral support on this and other projects, are always treasured.

Colleagues and students in Sicily, where much of this book was written, have also played an important role in this work, and I thank them for their very special friendships: Anna Reitano, Mary Puccia, Simona Barone, Giovanna Battaglia, Davide Fiorito, Simona Gambino, Antonella Gulino, Francesca Flaccavento, Rosaria Leone, and Giovanna Vernuccio.

In addition, I'd like to thank the following OUP staff for their support and assistance in the development of *Totally True*: Janet Aitchison, Oliver Bayley, Nick Bullard, Julia Chang, Tina Chen, Steven Ferguson, Satoko Fukazawa, JJ Lee, Constance Mo, Paul Riley, Amany Sarkiz, Julie Till, and Ted Yoshioka.

Finally, the publisher and the author would like to thank the following teachers whose comments, reviews, and assistance were instrumental in the development of *Totally True*: Young-sung Chueh, Kumiko Fushino, Paul Jen, Sue Kim, Yonghyun Kwon, Richard S. Lavin, Jong-Chul Seo, James Sims, Daniel Stewart, Ching-Yi Tien, Carol Vaughan, Lisa D. Vogt, Gerald Williams, and Mei-ling Wu.

1

Hello, My Name Is Scott

1. Read the story

Look at the pictures on these pages.
What is the story about? Now read it.

ST. LOUIS, USA   ¹One day, Scott Ginsberg, 23, went to a meeting* and put on a nametag**. It said, "Hello, my name is Scott." ²After the meeting, Scott forgot all about his nametag and **went out** to a **restaurant** with the nametag **still** on his shirt. ³**Strangers** were **friendly** to him and began **conversations**. "Hello, Scott!" they said. "What's up?***" Scott met 20 people that night and had a wonderful time.

⁴Now Scott wears a nametag all the time—at work and on weekends. ⁵He meets new people **everywhere**—at **parks**, movies, and supermarkets. ⁶"Most people want to be friendly," he says. "But they're afraid. Nametags **make** people **comfortable**. They break the **silence**, the **walls** between people."

---

  * meeting: when two or more people meet to talk
 ** nametag: a paper with your name that you put on
    a shirt or coat
*** What's up?: What's new?

NEW WORDS

go out v	**stranger** n	**everywhere** adv	**comfortable** adj
restaurant n	**friendly** adj	**park** n	**silence** n
still adv	**conversation** n	**make** v	**wall** n

>> See Glossary on page 88. >>

2. Rate the story

How much did you like it? Mark an ✗.

Not at All   A Lot
①　②　③　④　⑤

3. Check your comprehension

Put the sentences in the correct order. Number them 1–6. The first one is done for you.

a. ___ He now wears a nametag everywhere.

b. ___ Later, he went out to eat with the nametag still on.

c. ___ He had a wonderful time that night!

d. ___ He put on a nametag.

e. _1_ Scott Ginsberg went to a meeting.

f. ___ A lot of strangers talked to Scott.

4. Check your vocabulary

Complete the sentences with the New Words.

a. Scott forgot about his nametag and w_ _ _ out to a rest_ _ _ _ _ _.

b. St_ _ _ _ _ _s began _ _ _ _ersations with him.

c. Nametags, Scott says, m_ _ _ people com_ _ _ _ _ _ _ _.

d. Nametags break the sil_ _ _ _, the w_ _ _s between people.

5. Listen to the story   (•) track 2

Now listen to the story two or three times. Look at the pictures below as you listen.

6. Retell the story

Cover the story and look at the pictures above. Retell the story using the New Words.

7. Answer the questions

About the story…
a. What happened the first time Scott went out with his nametag on?
b. Where does Scott meet people now?
c. What does Scott say about nametags? What do they do?
d. What do you think? Are people afraid to be friendly?

About you…
e. Do you like to go out on weekends? Where?
f. Where do you meet new people?
g. How do you begin conversations with them?
h. How can we be more friendly?

8. Learn word partnerships

Study the partnerships below. Complete the sentences so they are true for you.

GO OUT			
go out	to	a restaurant a movie eat	**Scott went out to a restaurant.** *On weekends, Young-hee likes to go out to a movie.* *I don't often go out to eat at Burger Boy.*
	for	coffee dinner	*My friends love to go out for coffee.* *I went out for dinner yesterday with Ichiro.*

a. My friends and I like to go out _____.

b. I don't often _____ out _____.

c. I went _____ for _____ with _____.

9. Learn word groups

Complete the sentences so they are true for you. Use words from the pictures.

PLACES TO MEET FRIENDS

a cafe · a club · a movie theater · a restaurant · a shopping mall · a park

a. I like to meet my friends at _____.

b. We never meet at _____.

c. It's expensive to go out to _____ in my town.

4   Unit 1

10. Take a dictation ◉ track 3

Use your own paper to write the dictation. Check your answers on page 86.

11. Complete the story

Use the words from the box to complete the story.

everywhere	strangers	silence	make	parks	friendly

Say Hello!

ROTTERDAM, THE NETHERLANDS A Dutch politician* did not like the **(1)** _____ in Rotterdam. He wanted to **(2)** _____ people more **(3)** _____. So he put up a big sign** in Rotterdam. "Say Hello," the sign says.

The politician, Joel van der Meer, moved to Rotterdam last year. Before that, he lived in a small town in the north of the Netherlands. There, he says, people say hello to **(4)** _____ on the street, in cafes, and in **(5)** _____. "When I came to Rotterdam last year, I was shocked***. People here don't say hello on the street."

Van der Meer now wants to put up "Say Hello" signs **(6)** _____ in Rotterdam. "I want people to be friends," he says.

---

   * politician: someone who works in the government
  ** sign: a thing with writing or a picture on it that tells you something
*** shocked: very surprised

 Talk about the stories

How are the stories of Scott Ginsberg and Joel van der Meer similar? How are they different?

2 Python Boy

1. Read the story

Look at the pictures on these pages.
What is the story about? Now read it.

SIT TBOW, CAMBODIA **¹**Oeun Sambath, 3, has an **unusual** best friend. It is a **huge** python*— four meters long! **²**Oeun and his python, Lucky, are always **together**. **³**When they sleep, Lucky makes a big **circle** with his body. Little Oeun is in the **middle**, with his head on Lucky's head. **⁴**Oeun's mother is not **worried** about her son.

⁵Oeun gets a lot of visitors. "He's a **special** child," they say. "Maybe he was a son of a dragon** in his last **life**." **⁶**The boy does not like to be away from his **favorite** friend. Once the family took a **trip**, but they did not stay away long. "My son **missed** Lucky," said his mother. "So we came back early."

---

*python: a big, dangerous snake
**dragon: a big animal with fire in its mouth; it is not a real animal

NEW WORDS

unusual *adj*	circle *n*	special *adj*	trip *n*
huge *adj*	middle *n*	life *n*	miss *v*
together *adv*	worried *adj*	favorite *adj*	

>> See Glossary on page 88. >>

2. Rate the story

How much did you like it? Mark an ✗.

Not at All   A Lot
① ② ③ ④ ⑤

3. Check your comprehension

Check (✔) the endings that are true. The first one is done for you.

a. Oeun is

  ✓ a special child.

  ___ always with Lucky.

  ___ a dragon.

  ___ three years old.

b. Lucky is

  ___ a dragon.

  ___ a python.

  ___ Oeun's favorite friend.

  ___ very big.

4. Check your vocabulary

Complete the sentences with the New Words.

a. Lucky is a h_ _ _ and unu_ _ _ _ friend for a small boy.

b. Lucky makes a big ci_ _ _ _ with his body, and Oeun sleeps in the mi_ _ _ _.

c. Oeun sleeps with his head on Lucky's head, but his mother isn't wo_ _ _ _ _.

d. Oeun m_ _ _ed Lucky when the family took a t_ _ _.

5. Listen to the story track 4

Now listen to the story two or three times. Look at the pictures below as you listen.

6. Retell the story

Cover the story and look at the pictures above. Retell the story using the New Words.

7. Answer the questions

About the story…
a. How do the boy and the python sleep?
b. What do visitors say about the boy?
c. What happened when the family took a trip?
d. Would you like to meet Oeun or Lucky? Why or why not?

About you…
e. Who is your best friend? How often are you together?
f. What is your favorite animal? Why?
g. Where did you go on your last trip?
h. What do you miss most when you take a trip away from home?

8. Learn word partnerships

Study the partnerships below. Complete the sentences so they are true for you.

TRIP		
take plan	a trip	**Oeun's family took a trip.** We are planning a trip to Hong Kong in August.
a two-week a long/short an exciting	trip	Ming wants to take a two-week trip to Seoul. John is planning a short trip to Egypt. Last summer, I took an exciting trip to Kyoto.

a. I want to take _____.
b. My family is planning _____.
c. Last year, I _____ a _____ trip to _____.

9. Learn word groups

Complete the sentences so they are true for you. Use words from the picture.

SIZES

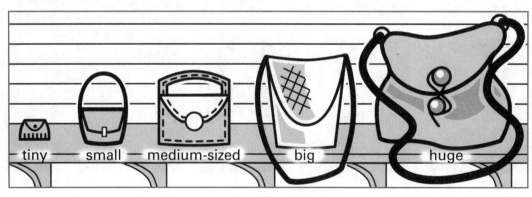

tiny — small — medium-sized — big — huge

a. I wear _____ shoes.
b. I would like to live in a _____ house.
c. I live in a _____ town, in a _____ country.

10. Take a dictation ⊙ track 5

Use your own paper to write the dictation. Check your answers on page 86.

11. Complete the story

Use the words from the box to complete the story.

worried	unusual	together	tiny	life	favorite

Monkey Is Woman's Best Friend

BOSTON, USA   Becky Thompson has a special best friend. She is a **(1)** _____ monkey*, and her name is Kristi. Kristi began to live with Thompson in 1998. Now they are always **(2)** _____. Thompson had an accident, and she cannot move her arms or legs. So Kristi does Thompson's hair. She helps her with the phone. She gets food** for Thompson and plays her **(3)** _____ CD.

   Thompson needs a lot of help, but she is not **(4)** _____. "Kristi helps me with everything. Before I had a monkey, my **(5)** _____ was in black and white. Now it is in color, and everything is good. She is my baby***." Monkeys are **(6)** _____ helpers, but nearly 100 people in the USA now have a monkey to help them.
_____

   *monkey: an animal with a long tail that can run up trees
  **food: people and animals eat food to live
***baby: a word that you use for someone you love

   Talk about the stories

Which animal would you like for a friend—a python or a monkey? Why?

3

Car-aoke

1. Read the story

Look at the pictures on these pages.
What is the story about? Now read it.

NINGBO, CHINA **1**Is there a lot of **traffic** in your town? Are the roads **busy**? Do you feel **bored** or angry **while** you sit in a long **line** of cars? **2**Then a **great**, new car from China can help! It is called the Geely Beauty Leopard*. **3**The car comes with a karaoke **machine**. You and your **passengers** can sing your favorite **pop songs** while you wait in traffic or take a trip. You **will** feel much better!

4The car has a GPS system** too, so you will never get lost. **5**The car **costs** about $18,000. **6**Be careful when you sing and drive at the same time. It can be **dangerous**. Watch the road and do not have an accident!

---

* Geely Beauty Leopard: the name of the car
** GPS system: a computerized map

NEW WORDS

traffic *n*	**bored** *adj*	**line** *n*	**machine** *n*	**pop song** *n*	**cost** *v*
busy *adj*	**while** *conj*	**great** *adj*	**passenger** *n*	**will** *v*	**dangerous** *adj*

>> See Glossary on page 89. >>

2. Rate the story

How much did you like it? Mark an ✗.

Not at All   A Lot

(1)   (2)   (3)   (4)   (5)

3. Check your comprehension

Match the first and second parts of the sentences. The first one is done for you.

a. The Geely Beauty Leopard has _3_

b. The car comes ___

c. Passengers can sing ___

d. With the GPS system, ___

e. The car costs ___

1. you won't get lost.

2. pop songs.

3. a karaoke machine.

4. thousands of dollars.

5. from China.

4. Check your vocabulary

Complete the sentences with the New Words.

a. Are the roads in your town bu_ _? Are you bo_ _ _ in traffic?

b. A gr_ _ _ new car from China has a karaoke mac_ _ _ _.

c. You and your pas_ _ _ _ _rs can sing p_ _ s_ _gs.

d. The car c_ _ _s about $18,000, and it can be dan_ _ _ _ _ _ when you sing and drive at the same time.

5. Listen to the story (•) track 6

Now listen to the story two or three times. Look at the pictures below as you listen.

6. Retell the story

Cover the story and look at the pictures above. Retell the story using the New Words.

7. Answer the questions

About the story…

a. What does the new car from China have?

b. How much does it cost? Do you think it is expensive?

c. When can it be dangerous?

d. Would you like to have this car? Why or why not?

About you…

e. What kind of car would you like?

f. How often do you sing karaoke? Where do you go?

g. What are your favorite pop songs?

h. When do you feel bored?

8. Learn word partnerships

Study the partnerships below. Complete the sentences so they are true for you.

COST			
cost	about more than only	($000.00)	**The car costs about $18,000.** A bicycle costs more than $100. Bus tickets cost only $2.00.
cost	a lot / too much a fortune		My CDs cost a lot. The trip will cost a fortune!

a. A new computer _____ about _____.

b. A _____ costs _____ in my country.

c. _____ cost only _____, so I often buy them.

9. Learn word groups

Complete the sentences so they are true for you. Use words from the pictures.

TRAFFIC

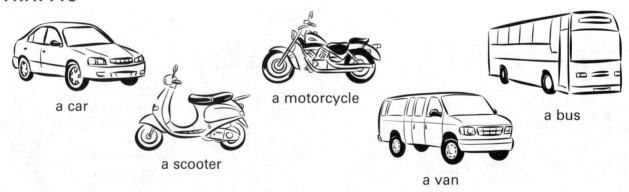

a car   a motorcycle   a bus

a scooter   a van

a. I'd like to drive _____.

b. I rode in/on _____ last week.

c. I don't often see _____ on the streets of my town.

10. Take a dictation track 7

Use your own paper to write the dictation. Check your answers on page 86.

11. Complete the story

Use the words from the box to complete the story.

vans	will	line	bored	while	machine	traffic

A Car with Feelings

JAPAN   In 2004, four workers at Toyota in Japan met and talked about new cars. "Let's make a car with feelings*," they said.

The car **(1)** _____ soon be on the road. The car with feelings will talk to cars and **(2)** _____ in traffic. The two lights** on the front of the **(3)** _____ are its eyes. When you are on the road and a driver is not nice to you, the car's eyes will go red and angry. When you want to say "thank you," you can make the car's eyes smile a happy yellow. **(4)** _____ you are sitting in a long **(5)** _____ of **(6)** _____ , your car can cry. How? Little white lights come on under its eyes.

The horn*** makes different noises for different feelings, too. Drivers can hear when you are happy, sorry, angry, friendly, or **(7)** _____.

---

  *feelings: something that you feel, like when you are happy
 **lights: things that help people see in the dark
***horn: something in a car that makes a loud noise (to warn)

  Talk about the stories

How are the cars in the two stories similar? How are they different? Which car do you like better?

4

Mud Day

1. Read the story

Look at the pictures on these pages.
What is the story about? Now read it.

WESTLAND, MICH., USA ¹Every July, the town of Westland has a **party**. It is exciting for everyone! ²The town puts 200,000 kilograms of **dirt** in a park. Then workers put 75,000 liters of water on the dirt. Suddenly there is a big sea of **mud**.

³A thousand children and **teenagers** run into the **soft** mud. ⁴Some try to **swim** in it. And some have mud **fights**. ⁵How do the dirty kids* get the mud off? First, **fire fighters wash** them with their hoses**, and then the **wet** kids go home and **take a bath**.

⁶Lauryn Jackson went to Mud Day this year with her younger brother. She **pushed** him into the mud and then put his face in it. "That was **fun**!" she said.

---

*kids (informal): children
**hoses: long, soft tubes that bring water to a fire

NEW WORDS

party *n*	**teenager** *n*	**fight** *n*	**wet** *adj*	**fun** *n*
dirt *n*	**soft** *adj*	**fire fighter** *n*	**take a bath** *v*	
mud *n*	**swim** *v*	**wash** *v*	**push** *v*	

>> See Glossary on page 89. >>

2. Rate the story

How much did you like it? Mark an ✗.

Not at All   A Lot
① ② ③ ④ ⑤

3. Check your comprehension

Correct five more mistakes in the story summary. The first one is done for you.

The town of Westland has an exciting party every ~~week~~ July. The town puts dirt in a park. Then workers put 75,000 liters of milk on the dirt. A thousand animals and teenagers sleep in the sea of mud and have a bad time. Lauryn Jackson went to Mud Day this year with her father. She pushed him into the mud. "That was fun!" she said.

4. Check your vocabulary

Complete the sentences with the New Words.

a. Every summer, Westland has a pa_ _ _ in a park.

b. Workers make a sea of m_ _ with lots of water and d_ _ _.

c. Children and teen_ _ _ _s have mud _ _ghts.

d. Lauryn Jackson p_ _ _ed her brother into the mud and then said, "That was f_ _!"

5. Listen to the story track 8

Now listen to the story two or three times. Look at the pictures below as you listen.

6. Retell the story

Cover the story and look at the pictures above. Retell the story using the New Words.

7. Answer the questions

About the story…
a. Why does the town of Westland make a sea of mud?
b. How do the workers make it?
c. What do the kids do in the mud?
d. How do they get the mud off?

About you…
e. Would you like to go to Mud Day? Why or why not?
f. What days in your town are fun?
g. What kind of parties do you like?
h. Where do you like to swim?

8. Learn word partnerships

Study the partnerships below. Complete the sentences so they are true for you.

FUN		
be have	fun	**"That was fun!" she said.** *I always have fun at Tom's parties.*
a lot of so much not much	fun	*Our trip to Hong Kong will be a lot of fun.* *My friends and I had so much fun at the park.* *I didn't have much fun at the restaurant.*

a. I always _____ fun at _____.
b. I don't have much fun _____.
c. _____ will be _____ fun.

9. Learn word groups

Complete the sentences so they are true for you. Use words from the pictures.

SUMMER ACTIVITIES

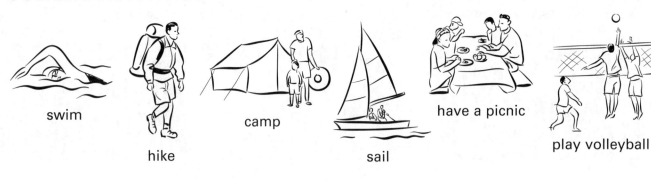

swim   hike   camp   sail   have a picnic   play volleyball

a. I often _____ in the summer, but I don't _____.
b. Next summer, I want to _____.
c. I learned to _____ when I was young.

10. Take a dictation ◎ track 9

Use your own paper to write the dictation. Check your answers on page 86.

11. Complete the story

Use the words from the box to complete the story.

| a lot of fun | take a bath | teenagers | wet | fights | party |

Wetter Is Better

CHIANG MAI, THAILAND Do you like water **(1)** _____? Then you will love visiting Thailand for *Songkran.* It is a big, watery **(2)** _____ for the Thai New Year in April.

Everywhere you go, people are laughing, playing in the streets, and throwing* water. In Chiang Mai, people stand in a line on the streets and throw water at cars and bikes. When you walk down the street, they hit you with water from hoses. **(3)** _____ throw water out of windows. The weather is hot, so the cold water feels good. Everyone has **(4)** _____!

When you go, dress comfortably and dress for fun. You will get **(5)** _____ from head to foot. So you will not need to **(6)** _____ that day!

*throwing: moving your arm fast and sending something into the air

 Talk about the stories

Would you like to go to Mud Day or *Songkran*? Which party do you think is more fun? Why?

5

His Mustache Pays

1. Read the story

Look at the pictures on these pages.
What is the story about? Now read it.

TURKEY **1**When you first see Mohammed Rashid, you are very **surprised**. You **have to** look again … and again! **2**Rashid, 62, has one of the longest **mustaches** in the **world**. It is 1.6 meters long, and it **flies** up into the **air** over his head, **like** two long **wings**. **3**Rashid loves his unusual mustache. Why? Because he is **traveling** the world and his beautiful mustache is **paying**.

4Rashid's wonderful **adventure** began in his country, Turkey. **5**In every new country, people walk up to him and want to take his photo. Rashid **lets** them—for five dollars a picture. **6**With the money from his mustache, Rashid pays for his trip—for hotels, **meals**, phone calls, trains, and planes. What a way to go!*

---

*What a way to go!: What an interesting trip!

NEW WORDS

surprised *adj*	world *n*	like *prep*	pay *v*	meal *n*
have to *v*	fly *v*	wing *n*	adventure *n*	
mustache *n*	air *n*	travel *v*	let *v*	

>> See Glossary on page 90. >>

2. Rate the story

How much did you like it? Mark an ✗.

Not at All   A Lot

① ② ③ ④ ⑤

3. Check your comprehension

Check (✔) the endings that are true.

a. Rashid has

___ an unusual mustache.

___ the longest hair in
the world.

b. Rashid's mustache

___ is two years old.

___ flies up into the air.

___ makes people look.

c. Rashid is traveling

___ to Turkey.

___ to many countries.

___ with money from his
mustache.

4. Check your vocabulary

Complete the sentences with the New Words.

a. When people see Rashid's mus_ _ _ _ _, they h_ _ _ to look again!

b. It flies up into the air, l_ _ _ two long w_ _ _s.

c. Rashid's adv_ _ _ _ _ _ began in Turkey.

d. Rashid's mustache p_ _s for his hotels and m_ _ _s.

5. Listen to the story track 10

Now listen to the story two or three times. Look at the pictures below as you listen.

6. Retell the story

Cover the story and look at the pictures above. Retell the story using the New Words.

7. Answer the questions

About the story…

a. How is Rashid's mustache unusual?

b. What adventure is Rashid having?

c. What things does his mustache pay for?

d. Would you like to meet Rashid? What question do you have for him?

About you…

e. Would you like to travel the world? Where would you go?

f. What adventure will you always remember?

g. What photos do you like to take?

h. Where do you eat your meals?

8. Learn word partnerships

Study the partnerships below. Complete the sentences so they are true for you.

PAY		
pay	for something	**Rashid pays for his trips with his mustache.**
		I pay for my meals every day.
	a lot for something	*Akemi paid a lot for her computer.*
pay	a bill	*She pays three bills every month.*
	the rent	*I should pay my rent soon.*

a. I pay for _____ and _____ every week.

b. I paid a lot _____.

c. My father _____ for his _____.

9. Learn word groups

Complete the sentences so they are true for you. Use words from the pictures.

MEALS

| breakfast | brunch | lunch | dinner | a snack |

a. My favorite meal is _____.

b. Sometimes I don't eat _____.

c. My biggest meal is _____.

10. Take a dictation ○ track 11

Use your own paper to write the dictation. Check your answers on page 86.

11. Complete the story

Use the words from the box to complete the story.

meals	world	adventure	surprised	traveled	paid for	let

Woman, 101, Sees China in a Pedicab

HARBIN, CHINA For three and a half years, Yimin Wang and his 101-year-old mother **(1)** _____ from town to town in China. They went 20,000 kilometers across the huge country. Strangers were always **(2)** _____ to see them. Why? Because Wang, 76, was pulling* his mother in a pedicab**!

Their **(3)** _____ began in Harbin in May 2000. In the next three and a half years, they saw most of China. They **(4)** _____ the trip with $6,800 of their savings***. When they had no more money, strangers gave them free **(5)** _____ and **(6)** _____ them stay in their homes.

In December 2003, the two of them went home because Wang's mother got sick. She died soon after. "I wanted her to see the **(7)** _____," said Wang.

_____

* pulling: moving something behind you
** pedicab: a bicycle that pulls a passenger
*** savings: money that you put away for later

 Talk about the stories

How are the adventures of Mohammed Rashid and Yimin Wang similar? How are they different? Which man would you most like to meet? Why?

6

Man Wants People to Laugh

1. Read the story

Look at the pictures on these pages.
What is the story about? Now read it.

SOUTH AMERICA [1]In 2001, Alvaro Neil, a Spanish **lawyer**, left his important **job** and **sold** his nice car. [2]Then he got on a plane and flew to South America to **follow** his **heart**. "I'm going to be a clown* on a bike!" he said. "I want people to laugh. I want them to be happy."

[3]Now Neil is **riding** his bike all the **way** across ten South American countries. [4]He travels from town to town **by himself** and carries everything on his bike—a **tent**, a bed, and his clown **clothes**. [5]Neil is **funny**, and he **performs** for free—for children and **adults**. [6]"People often forget to laugh," he says, "but it's very important! Work isn't everything in life."

---

*clown: someone who makes people laugh

NEW WORDS

lawyer *n*	follow *v*	way *n*	clothes *n*	adult *n*
job *n*	heart *n*	by oneself *adv*	funny *adj*	
sell *v*	ride *v*	tent *n*	perform *v*	

>> See Glossary on page 90. >>

2. Rate the story

How much did you like it? Mark an ✗.

Not at All   A Lot

① — ② — ③ — ④ — ⑤

3. Check your comprehension

Correct five mistakes in the story summary.

Alvaro Neil, a Spanish doctor, left his good job and flew to North America to follow his heart. "I'm going to be a clown on a bus!" he said. Now Neil is riding through ten countries. He carries everything with him on his bike—his tent, his car, and his clown clothes. "People often forget to cry," he says, "but it's very important!"

4. Check your vocabulary

Complete the sentences with the New Words.

a. Neil was a law_ _ _, but he left his j_ _ and s_ _ _ his car.

b. He wanted to fo_ _ _ _ his he_ _ _ and be a clown.

c. He travels by h_ _ _ _ _ _, and he carries his te_ _ and his clown clo_ _ _ _.

d. Neil per_ _ _ _s for ad_ _ _s and children.

5. Listen to the story track 12

Now listen to the story two or three times. Look at the pictures below as you listen.

6. Retell the story

Cover the story and look at the pictures above. Retell the story using the New Words.

7. Answer the questions

About the story...

a. Why did Neil leave his job as a lawyer?

b. How and where is he traveling in South America?

c. What does he carry with him?

d. Who does he perform for?

About you...

e. Would you like a funny friend like Neil? Why or why not?

f. What makes you laugh?

g. Which job would you like better—clown or lawyer? Why?

h. What are the three most important things in your life?

8. Learn word partnerships

Study the partnerships below. Complete the sentences so they are true for you.

RIDE		
ride	a bike	**Neil is riding his bike through South America.**
	a horse	*I rode a horse last summer.*
	a scooter	*I would like to ride a scooter to class.*
	a motorcycle	*Be careful when you ride your motorcycle.*
	a bus	*Young-hee rides a bus to work every day.*

a. I would like to ride _____ sometime.

b. I sometimes ride _____ to _____.

c. I rode _____.

9. Learn word groups

Complete the sentences so they are true for you. Use words from the pictures.

JOBS

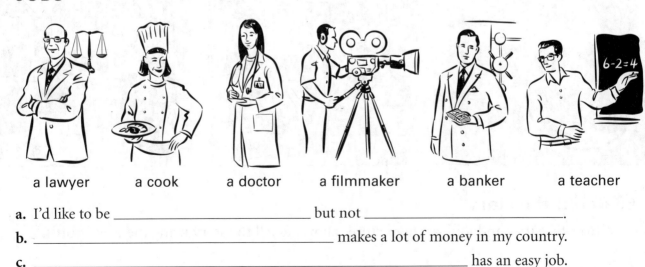

a lawyer   a cook   a doctor   a filmmaker   a banker   a teacher

a. I'd like to be _____ but not _____.

b. _____ makes a lot of money in my country.

c. _____ has an easy job.

10. Take a dictation 🔘 track 13

Use your own paper to write the dictation. Check your answers on page 86.

11. Complete the story

Use the words from the box to complete the story.

bankers	adults	funny	jobs	by yourself	perform

Woman Wants People to Laugh

BRUSSELS, BELGIUM "People need to laugh more," says Catherine Rochigneux of Brussels. She began a laughter club* because she wanted to make people feel better. Her club meets every day for a long, 15-minute laugh. "It's like a party," she says. The club is open to all **(1)** _____.

You can find laughter clubs everywhere–in Singapore, India, Canada, and Australia. There are hundreds of these clubs in the USA. A bank** in Osaka, Japan, opened a laughter club, too. **(2)** _____ people **(3)** _____ there and make the **(4)** _____ laugh. So they like their **(5)** _____ better now. "This is a happy bank," says the director***.

It is fun to laugh, but it is hard to do it **(6)** _____. Clubs like Catherine's can help.

_____

*laughter club: a place where people meet to laugh
**bank: a place that puts people's money away
***director: the head of a bank or a company

 Talk about the stories

What new things did you learn in this unit? What happens when you laugh?

1. Match the words with the pictures.

___ **a.** tent   ___ **d.** middle

___ **b.** party   ___ **e.** park

___ **c.** restaurant   ___ **f.** fire fighter

1.
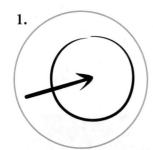

2.
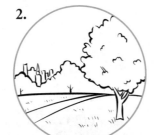

3.

4.

5.

6.

2. Write the words in the picture.

| traffic | wall | mustache | circle | teenager | wing |

3. Are the sentences true or false? Check (✓) the correct box.

	T	F
a. Computers and planes are machines.	☐	☐
b. Cars fly in the air.	☐	☐
c. Teenagers are older than adults.	☐	☐
d. When you put a lot of water on dirt, you get mud.	☐	☐
e. Breakfast is a morning meal.	☐	☐
f. You get wet when you swim.	☐	☐

4. Circle the item that completes each sentence.

a. I was very _____ on the car trip because the road was dangerous.

    1. friendly   2. comfortable   3. worried   4. bored

b. How much did your new camera _____?

    1. cost   2. pay   3. sell   4. miss

c. Fu-an works in a restaurant now, but he wants to be a _____.

    1. job   2. passenger   3. lawyer   4. stranger

d. Pam and Yasmin love to sing pop songs, and they often perform _____.

    1. special   2. busy   3. fun   4. together

e. Nobody was talking; there was only _____.

    1. air   2. silence   3. a circle   4. an adventure

5. Match the words with the definitions.

a. sell ____	1. all the cars, etc., on the road
b. job ____	2. the part in the center
c. travel ____	3. nice to people
d. middle ____	4. the work that you do for money
e. friendly ____	5. someone in a car who is not driving
f. traffic ____	6. to give something to someone who pays you for it
g. great ____	7. to go from one place to another
h. passenger ____	8. very good; wonderful

6. Use the words from the box to complete the sentences.

machine	soft	by himself	mustache	strangers
push	special	like	line	life	still	heart

a. Scott Ginsberg _____ wears a nametag every day, and he meets _____ everywhere.

b. "Oeun is a _____ child, " people say. "Maybe he was a son of a dragon in his last _____."

c. The Geely Beauty Leopard comes with a karaoke _____. You can sing while you sit in a long _____ of traffic!

d. On Mud Day, children swim in the _____ mud and _____ their friends into it.

e. Mohammed Rashid's _____ flies up into the air _____ two long wings.

f. Alvaro Neil followed his _____ and is now riding his bike _____ across South America.

7. Use the words from the box to complete the story.

made	surprised	way	while
unusual	soft	had to	

Dad Drives Snow to Son

TOTTON, ENGLAND When Elliot O'Sullivan was two years old, he badly wanted to see snow* and play in it. He cried and cried when no snow arrived that winter.

His father, Shaun O'Sullivan, was working 175 kilometers away from home in Kent, and there was a lot of snow there. So Shaun did something **(1)** _____. He put big boxes of snow in his car and took them home. His car windows stayed open **(2)** _____ he drove because the snow **(3)** _____ stay cold! It was a long **(4)** _____, and Shaun was cold and not very comfortable.

When little Elliot saw his father and all the **(5)** _____, white snow in the car, he was **(6)** _____ and excited. "It was wonderful!" said Shaun. "I **(7)** _____ him happy."

*snow: soft, white stuff that falls from the sky when it is cold

8. Check (✓) *yes* or *no*.

		Yes	No
a.	I am always very busy.	☐	☐
b.	I have some funny friends.	☐	☐
c.	I ride a bus to school or work.	☐	☐
d.	There is a lot of traffic in my town.	☐	☐

		Yes	No
e.	I like to study and read in silence.	☐	☐
f.	My teacher makes us work hard.	☐	☐
g.	I want to travel the world.	☐	☐
h.	I love singing pop songs!	☐	☐

9. Complete the sentences so they are true for you.

a. My favorite food is _____.

b. Every week I pay for _____ and _____.

c. I like having conversations with _____.

d. I'm bored when (I have to) _____.

e. I had a fight with _____.

f. Every day I have to _____ and _____.

g. I was very surprised when _____.

h. When I leave home for more than a day, I miss _____.

i. When I was a child, my mother let me _____.

10. Fill in the chart with names of classmates. Try to write a different name in each blank. Walk around the room and ask questions such as:

Will you go out to a restaurant tonight?
Did you go to a party last weekend?

The winner is the first person to fill in seven blanks.

FIND SOMEONE WHO...

a. will go out to a restaurant tonight. _____

b. went to a party last weekend. _____

c. has a lot of fun on weekends. _____

d. likes to swim every day. _____

e. washed some clothes yesterday. _____

f. often rides a bike. _____

g. had a great adventure last summer. _____

h. wants to live in a huge house. _____

i. took a bath yesterday. _____

j. is comfortable when he/she speaks English. _____

7

Tall Hair

1. Read the story

Look at the pictures on these pages.
What is the story about? Now read it.

SANTA FE, USA **¹**Long hair usually **hangs** down, but Lexie Osburn's **straight** hair stands up. **²**People are surprised to see her, Lexie says, but they say **kind** things about her hairstyle*. "It's beautiful **art**," an old woman said to her once on the street. **³**And what do her mother and father say? "My mom is OK with it," Lexie says, "but my dad doesn't want to go out with me **anywhere**."

⁴Lexie can do her hair in about 90 minutes. She uses gel** on it. This **keeps** it straight. When the gel **dries**, the hair stands tall. **⁵**Sometimes she **cuts** the **sides** or puts color on it—**purple** or blue. **⁶**But there is one **problem** with her hair. "When it's **windy**," she says, "it goes **flat**."

*hairstyle: how you do your hair
**gel: you put this on your hair to make it hard

NEW WORDS

hang *v*	art *n*	keep *v*	side *n*	windy *adj*
straight *adj*	anywhere *adv*	dry *v*	purple *adj*	flat *adj*
kind *adj*	use *v*	cut *v*	problem *n*	

>> See Glossary on page 91. >>

2. Rate the story

How much did you like it? Mark an ✗.

Not at All   A Lot
① ② ③ ④ ⑤

3. Check your comprehension

Match the first and second parts of the sentences.

a. Lexie puts ___   1. nice things about Lexie's hair.

b. Sometimes she cuts ___   2. OK with her daughter's hairstyle.

c. Her hair goes ___   3. want to go anywhere with Lexie.

d. People say ___   4. the sides of her hair.

e. Lexie's mother is ___   5. gel on her hair.

f. Her father doesn't ___   6. flat when it's windy.

4. Check your vocabulary

Complete the sentences with the New Words.

a. Most long hair h_ _ _s down, but Lexie's str_ _ _ _ _ hair stands up.

b. Lexie's hair is like a_ _, and people say k_ _ _ things to her.

c. Lexie u_ _s gel on her hair. When it d_ _es, her hair stands tall.

d. Sometimes she c_ _s the s_ _ _s of her hair.

5. Listen to the story   track 14

Now listen to the story two or three times. Look at the pictures below as you listen.

6. Retell the story

Cover the story and look at the pictures above. Retell the story using the New Words.

7. Answer the questions

About the story…

a. How is Lexie's hair different?

b. How does she keep it straight?

c. What does her father think of her hair?

d. What do you think of it?

About you…

e. What is your favorite hairstyle and hair color?

f. How much time do you take to wash, dry, and do your hair?

g. Do your family and friends like your hair and clothes? Why or why not?

h. What hairstyle and clothes do you see everywhere now? What did you see last year?

8. Learn word partnerships

Study the partnerships below. Complete the sentences so they are true for you.

PROBLEM		
There is a **problem** (with something)	*There is one problem with Lexie's hair.*	
have a **problem** (with something)	*I always have a problem with my phone.*	
a small a big	problem	*There's a small problem with your homework.* *Mei-ling had a big problem with her computer.*

a. I often _____ a problem with _____.

b. There is a _____ problem _____ in my town.

c. Last week, I _____ problem _____.

9. Learn word groups

Complete the sentences so they are true for you. Use words from the pictures.

HAIR

straight hair   wavy hair   curly hair   spiky hair   braids   a buzz cut

a. I like _____.

b. When I was ten years old, I had _____.

c. My best friend has _____.

10. Take a dictation 🔘 track 15

Use your own paper to write the dictation. Check your answers on page 86.

11. Complete the story

Use the words from the box to complete the story.

| problem | kind | cut | wavy | buzz cut | kept | hung |

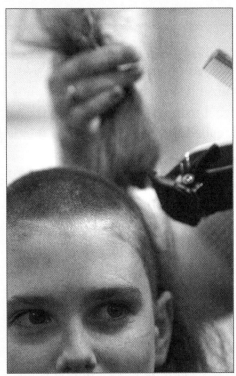

SEATTLE, USA   For months Dominic Bizak, 11, grew* his beautiful, dark, **(1)** _____ hair. Every day it got longer and longer. Boys in his class were not **(2)** _____ to him. "Are you a girl?" they cried.

"My hair was a big **(3)** _____ for me," Dominic says. "People said bad things." But Dominic **(4)** _____ his long hair, and after nearly two years, it **(5)** _____ down past his shoulders**.

Dominic did not want to **(6)** _____ his hair because he wanted to do something for charity***. There are many sick children without hair, and Dominic wanted to give his beautiful, long hair to one of those children.

When Dominic cut his hair after two years, he got a flat **(7)** _____, like most of the boys in his class. "I helped a stranger," Dominic says, "and I feel happy."

_____

* grew: let it get longer
** shoulders: the part of your body between your neck and your arms
*** charity: a group that collects money and other things to help people

 Talk about the stories

Imagine that you and a partner are Lexie Osburn and Dominic Bizak. You are meeting for the first time. Tell each other about your hairstyles.

8

Man Flies like a Bird

1. Read the story

Look at the pictures on these pages.
What is the story about? Now read it.

ENGLAND AND FRANCE ¹Would you like to fly through the air like a **bird**, with your very **own** wings? ²In 2003, Felix Baumgartner did! The Austrian man put on a suit with wings and **jumped** out of a plane over England. ³His wings **caught** the **wind**, and he flew **above** the English Channel at 220 kilometers an hour. He got to France in **just** 14 minutes. ⁴Then he opened his parachute* and went down near the French town of Calais.

⁵Felix, 34, is the first **person** to fly across the Channel without an **engine**. Felix loves to fly. "It's just you, the sky, and your wings," he says. ⁶An Austrian **business** will soon sell the suit with wings, called a Skyray, so maybe this will be a **popular sport** some day!

*parachute: a thing like a big umbrella that you use when you jump out of a plane

NEW WORDS

bird *n*	**jump** *v*	**wind** *n*	**just** *adv*	**engine** *n*	**popular** *adj*
own *adj*	**catch** *v*	**above** *prep*	**person** *n*	**business** *n*	**sport** *n*

>> See Glossary on page 91. >>

2. Rate the story

How much did you like it? Mark an ✗.

Not at All   A Lot

① ② ③ ④ ⑤

3. Check your comprehension

Put the sentences in the correct order. Number them 1–6.

a. ___ When he was above France, he opened his parachute.

b. ___ Felix Baumgartner got into a plane with a Skyray suit on.

c. ___ He flew like a bird over the English Channel.

d. ___ Somewhere over England, he jumped out.

e. ___ He went down near Calais, France.

f. ___ The wings on his suit caught the wind.

4. Check your vocabulary

Complete the sentences with the New Words.

a. Felix was the first pe_ _ _ _ to fly across the English Channel without an en_ _ _ _.

b. He j_ _ _ed out of a plane and flew with his very o_ _ wings.

c. Felix loves to catch the w_ _ _ and fly. "It's j_ _ _ you, the sky, and your wings," he says.

d. An Austrian bus_ _ _ _ _ _ will soon sell the Skyray.

5. Listen to the story   track 16

Now listen to the story two or three times. Look at the pictures below as you listen.

6. Retell the story

Cover the story and look at the pictures above. Retell the story using the New Words.

7. Answer the questions

About the story…

a. How did Felix fly across the English Channel?

b. How long did it take? How fast did Felix fly?

c. How and where did he land?

d. What else do you know about Felix?

About you…

e. What questions would you like to ask Felix?

f. Would you like to fly like a bird with a Skyray suit on? Why or why not?

g. Would you like to jump out of a plane with a parachute?

h. What dangerous or popular sports would you like to do?

8. Learn word partnerships

Study the partnerships below. Complete the sentences so they are true for you.

SPORT		
a popular		*Maybe this will soon be a popular sport!*
a fun		*Baseball is a fun sport.*
a boring	sport	*Golf is a boring sport, I think.*
an exciting		*I like basketball because it is an exciting sport.*
an easy		*Skiing is an easy sport.*

a. _____ is a popular sport in my country.

b. Soccer is _____ sport, I think.

c. I like _____ because it is _____.

9. Learn word groups

Complete the sentences so they are true for you. Use words from the pictures.

BIRDS

an owl   a duck   a crow   a pigeon   an eagle   a crane

a. I often see _____.

b. _____ is more beautiful than _____.

c. My favorite bird is _____.

10. Take a dictation track 17

Use your own paper to write the dictation. Check your answers on page 86.

11. Complete the story

Use the words from the box to complete the story.

catch   engine   above   bird   wind   sport   cranes

Man Wants to Be a Bird

RUSSIA AND NEPAL Angelo d'Arrigo is learning to think and fly like a **(1)** _____. "He wants to *be* a bird," some people say.

The Italian man often flies with birds in his hang glider*. In 2002, he flew over Siberia with six young **(2)** _____. The beautiful birds are endangered**, and they were learning to fly to a new winter home. Like a father, d'Arrigo flew under the cranes. They followed **(3)** _____ his wings.

At night, d'Arrigo and the birds ate and slept together. In the morning, d'Arrigo used the small **(4)** _____ on his hang glider to get back into the sky. He stopped it when the glider began to **(5)** _____ the **(6)** _____. Together, the seven "birds" traveled 1,500 kilometers.

In 2004, d'Arrigo flew over Mount Everest with an eagle. The man loves his **(7)** _____ but more importantly, his birds.

_____

*hang glider: something like a kite that someone can hang from
**endangered: when an animal is endangered, there are not many alive

 Talk about the stories

Imagine that you and a partner are Felix Baumgartner and Angelo d'Arrigo. You are meeting for the first time. Tell each other about your adventures.

9

32 Days with Scorpions

1. Read the story

Look at the pictures on these pages.
What is the story about? Now read it.

PATTAYA, THAILAND **1**For 32 days, Kanchana Ketkeaw, 30, lived **inside** a very big **glass** box in a shop in Thailand. She left it for **only** 15 minutes every eight hours when she took a bath. **2**She lived **alone** in her glass room, with only a bed, a TV, **newspapers**, and a **refrigerator**. **3**And 3,400 dangerous scorpions*! The little animals **climbed** everywhere—on the bed, up the walls, and over the **floor**. "It was like my room at home," she said later, "but with thousands of little friends."

4Shoppers and **tourists** stopped and watched. Kanchana, an **artist**, often performs with scorpions. **5**Nine scorpions stung** Kanchana this time, but she wasn't afraid. **6**She gave them good **food**—usually **eggs** and meat. Some scorpions died and **other** scorpions were born in her 32 days with them.

---

*scorpions: small animals with six legs and a long tail
**stung: hurt by pushing a small, sharp part into your skin

NEW WORDS

inside prep	**alone** adv	**climb** v	**artist** n	**other** det
glass n	**newspaper** n	**floor** n	**food** n	
only adv	**refrigerator** n	**tourist** n	**egg** n	

>> See Glossary on page 92. >>

2. Rate the story

How much did you like it? Mark an ✗.

Not at All   A Lot
(1)   (2)   (3)   (4)   (5)

---

3. Check your comprehension

Check (✔) the endings that are true.

a. Kanchana

____ never left the glass room for 32 days.

____ had a refrigerator in her room.

____ climbed up the walls of her glass box.

____ is an artist.

b. The scorpions

____ took a bath every day.

____ stung Kanchana.

____ ate eggs and meat.

____ stayed away from Kanchana.

4. Check your vocabulary

Complete the sentences with the New Words.

a. Kanchana lived ins_ _ _ a big gl_ _ _ box in a shop in Thailand.

b. She was al_ _ _ for 32 days, with only some news_ _ _ _rs, a TV, and 3,400 scorpions!

c. Many shoppers and to_ _ _ _ts stopped to watch the art_ _ _.

d. Some scorpions were born and ot_ _ _ scorpions died in her 32 days with them.

5. Listen to the story   ⊙ track 18

Now listen to the story two or three times. Look at the pictures below as you listen.

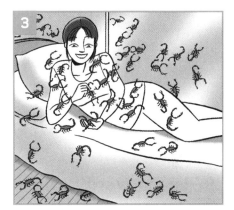

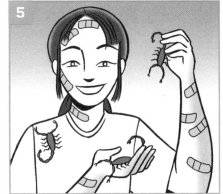

6. Retell the story

Cover the story and look at the pictures above. Retell the story using the New Words.

7. Answer the questions

About the story…

a. What was inside Kanchana's glass room?

b. Why did she live there for 32 days?

c. Who watched her?

d. What happened to some of the scorpions?

About you…

e. What question would you like to ask Kanchana?

f. Would you like to be an artist like her? Why or why not?

g. Are you afraid of any animals? Which ones?

h. What do you have in your room at home?

8. Learn word partnerships

Study the partnerships below. Complete the sentences so they are true for you.

FOOD		
good/bad		**Kanchana gave the scorpions good food.**
delicious		*What delicious food this is!*
spicy		*My family eats spicy food at restaurants.*
healthy/unhealthy	food	*He eats a lot of unhealthy food.*
junk		*I don't like soda and junk food.*
vegetarian		*My favorite vegetarian food is noodles with tofu.*

a. I eat a lot of _____ food and not much _____ food.

b. My favorite _____ food is _____.

c. I like to eat _____ at restaurants.

9. Learn word groups

Complete the sentences so they are true for you. Use words from the picture.

A ROOM

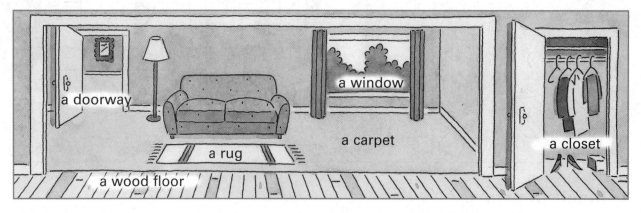

a doorway

a window

a carpet

a rug

a wood floor

a closet

a. There is _____ in my room, but it's not very big.

b. There is _____ near my bed.

c. I don't have _____ in my room.

10. Take a dictation track 19

Use your own paper to write the dictation. Check your answers on page 86.

11. Complete the story

Use the words from the box to complete the story.

only	refrigerator	inside	climb	floor	food

An Unusual Pet

CANBERRA, AUSTRALIA   Many people want a pet*. But some people **(1)** _____ have a small home, with no room **(2)** _____ for a dog or a cat. What can they do? They can get a cockroach**!

Cockroaches are more and more popular. "Yes, they are unusual pets," says John Olive, a worker in Australia's pet business. "But they are easy pets and not much work."

Pet cockroaches are not those little animals on the **(3)** _____ and walls behind your **(4)** _____. These cockroaches are huge—about four centimeters long and very fat. They have no wings, so they cannot fly. And they are not dirty.

The animals learn well, says Steve Austin, a cockroach lover in Australia. They can **(5)** _____ over little hills and get their **(6)** _____. And they can come to you when you call their name!
_____

*pet: an animal that you keep in your home
**cockroach: an insect that lives in homes and comes out at night

 Talk about the stories

Which story is more surprising? Which one did you like better? Why?

10

Reaching to the Sky

1. Read the story

Look at the pictures on these pages.
What is the story about? Now read it.

TAIPEI, TAIWAN ¹Taipei 101, the world's **highest** building, opened in 2004 after six years of work. With 101 **floors**, it stands tall above the other buildings in Taipei—a half kilometer tall! ²"Tapei 101 **reaches** to the sky like a **plant**," says one of the architects*, C. P. Wang.

³Taipei 101 has eight sections**, a **lucky** number for the Chinese. ⁴It is **also** very **strong**. Taiwan often has **earthquakes** and strong winds, but they cannot **damage** it. ⁵The **elevators** are the fastest and most **modern** in the world. They travel at 60 kilometers per hour. You arrive on the 91st floor in 39 seconds, and from there you can look out over Taipei.

⁶**By** 2008, Seoul will have a taller building. But for now, Taipei 101 is Number One.

---

*architects: people who have the job of planning buildings
**sections: parts of something

NEW WORDS

high *adj*	**plant** *n*	**strong** *adj*	**elevator** *n*
floor *n*	**lucky** *adj*	**earthquake** *n*	**modern** *adj*
reach *v*	**also** *adv*	**damage** *v*	**by** *prep*

>> See Glossary on page 92. >>

2. Rate the story

How much did you like it? Mark an ✗.

Not at All   A Lot
① ② ③ ④ ⑤

3. Check your comprehension

Correct five mistakes in the story summary.

Taipei 101 is the world's tallest plant. It's a half kilometer tall! Taipei 101 has eight sections and ten floors. It is weak, and earthquakes cannot damage it. The elevators are modern and slow. You can go to the 91st floor and see all of Taiwan.

4. Check your vocabulary

Complete the sentences with the New Words.

a. With 101 f_ _ _rs, Taipei 101 is a very h_ _ _ building!

b. Eight is a l_ _ _ _ number for the Chinese.

c. Earthquakes will not da_ _ _ _ the building because it is st_ _ _ _.

d. B_ 2008, Seoul will al_ _ have a very tall building.

5. Listen to the story ⊙ track 20

Now listen to the story two or three times. Look at the pictures below as you listen.

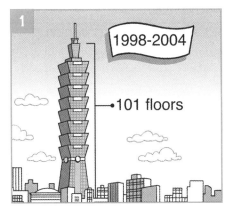
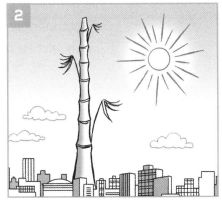

6. Retell the story

Cover the story and look at the pictures above. Retell the story using the New Words.

7. Answer the questions

About the story…

a. What does the architect say about Taipei 101?
b. Why must the building be strong?
c. How fast do the elevators move?
d. Would you like to go up Taipei 101? Why or why not?

About you…

e. What is the tallest building in your town? In your country?
f. How high do you think buildings will get by 2020?
g. Do you have earthquakes or strong winds in your country? How often?
h. Would you like to be an architect? Why or why not?

8. Learn word partnerships

Study the partnerships below. Complete the sentences so they are true for you.

STRONG			
a very		building	***Taipei 101 is a very strong building.***
a really	strong	wind	*We had really strong winds!*
an extremely		person	*My grandfather is an extremely strong person.*
an unusually		earthquake	*Turkey had an unusually strong earthquake.*

a. My _____ is _____ strong person.
b. We had _____ last year.
c. _____ is _____ building.

9. Learn word groups

Complete the sentences so they are true for you. Use words from the picture.

IN A BUILDING

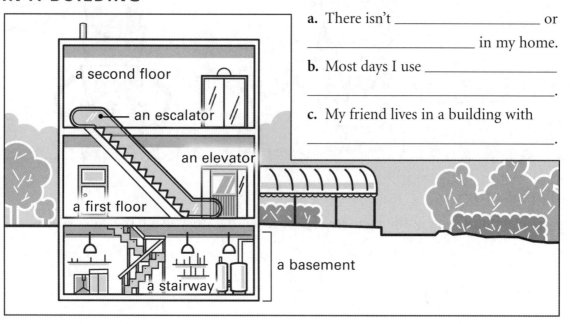

a second floor
an escalator
an elevator
a first floor
a stairway
a basement

a. There isn't _____ or _____ in my home.

b. Most days I use _____ _____.

c. My friend lives in a building with _____.

10. Take a dictation 🔘 track 21

Use your own paper to write the dictation. Check your answers on page 86.

11. Complete the story

Use the words from the box to complete the story.

| modern | lucky | stairway | extremely strong winds | highest | damage | elevator |

"Monstrous" Building Is Now World Famous

PARIS, FRANCE   One hundred years ago, the Eiffel Tower* was the **(1)** _____ building in the world. But when it opened in 1889, after just two years of work, it was not popular with Parisians. "It's monstrous**!" said angry French artists about the **(2)** _____ building.

   But slowly, Parisians learned to love the tower, and today they feel **(3)** _____. It is in the middle of Paris and a work of art. Every year, six million tourists visit this very popular building in Europe. Take the **(4)** _____ or walk up the very long **(5)** _____, and then you can see all of Paris at your feet.

   (6) _____ sometimes hit Paris. But Parisians are not worried. The winds cannot **(7)** _____ the famous building. Two and a half million rivets*** keep it together.

_____

*tower: a high, narrow building
**monstrous: big and ugly
***rivets: small pieces of metal that hold two things together

 Talk about the stories

How are Taipei 101 and the Eiffel Tower similar? How are they different? Which one would you most like to visit? Why?

11

His Car Is His Kitchen

1. Read the story

Look at the pictures on these pages.
What is the story about? Now read it.

OSLO, NORWAY ¹Do you like to **cook**? Kyrre Johansen, 40, loves to. But he does not cook meals in his **kitchen** the **way** most other people do. Ten years ago, he began to cook **on top of** the hot engine of his car!

²When he takes a long car trip, Johansen often cooks steak* or **fish**. ³On **short** trips, he can make hot dogs** for his children. ⁴It is a **strange** way to cook, Johansen **agrees**, but he says, "My meat is **so** soft, and it **tastes** so good!" ⁵He puts the meat in foil*** before he cooks it. That way, it will not **smell** like **gas**. ⁶Johansen is busy. He **saves** time when he drives and cooks at the same time. When he gets home from work, dinner is ready!

---

*steak: a thick piece of meat, usually from a cow
**hot dogs: frankfurters (meat) inside bread
***foil: metal that is very thin like paper; you use it to cover food

NEW WORDS

cook v	**on top of** prep	**strange** adj	**taste** v	**save** v
kitchen n	**fish** n	**agree** v	**smell** v	
way n	**short** adj	**so** adv	**gas** n	

>> See Glossary on page 93. >>

2. Rate the story

How much did you like it? Mark an ✗.

Not at All   A Lot
① ② ③ ④ ⑤

3. Check your comprehension

Match the first and second parts of the sentences.

a. Most people cook ___
b. Johansen makes ___
c. His meat tastes ___
d. It doesn't smell ___
e. He saves ___

1. very good.
2. like gas.
3. in the kitchen.
4. a lot of time when he drives and cooks.
5. meals on his car engine.

4. Check your vocabulary

Complete the sentences with the New Words.

a. Johansen makes f_ _ _ on t_ _ of his car engine.
b. It's a strange w_ _ to cook, Johansen ag_ _ _s.
c. He cooks the food in foil. That way it won't sm_ _ _ like g_ _.
d. Johansen s_ _ _s time because he c_ _ _s and drives at the same time.

5. Listen to the story track 22

Now listen to the story two or three times. Look at the pictures below as you listen.

6. Retell the story

Cover the story and look at the pictures above. Retell the story using the New Words.

7. Answer the questions

About the story…

a. How is Johansen different from other people?

b. How does he cook his food?

c. What does he cook on short trips? On long trips?

d. Would you like to eat Johansen's food? Why or why not?

About you…

e. What do you like to eat for lunch or dinner?

f. What two things do you do at the same time?

g. Are you busy? How do you save time?

h. How often do you take car trips? Where do you go?

8. Learn word partnerships

Study the partnerships below. Complete the sentences so they are true for you.

TASTE			
something **tastes** (so)	good	**Johansen's meat tastes so good!**	
	great	The cake tastes great.	
	strange	The sandwich tastes strange.	
	bad	Milk tastes bad, I think.	
	awful	That hamburger tastes so awful!	

a. Steak tastes _____, I think.

b. _____ tastes strange!

c. Chocolate cake _____.

9. Learn word groups

Complete the sentences so they are true for you. Use words from the pictures.

IN THE KITCHEN

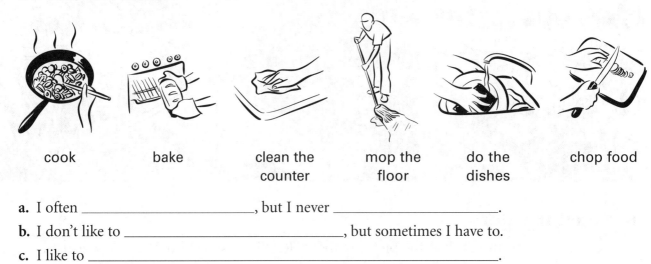

cook   bake   clean the   mop the   do the   chop food
                            counter   floor   dishes

a. I often _____, but I never _____.

b. I don't like to _____, but sometimes I have to.

c. I like to _____.

10. Take a dictation   track 23

Use your own paper to write the dictation. Check your answers on page 87.

11. Complete the story

Use the words from the box to complete the story.

on top of	short	agrees	smells	strange	so

His Car Is His Garden

MIAMI, USA   Keith Moss loves plants. So he did something **(1)** _____. He put chicken wire* over his old car and then put plants under the chicken wire. Big, beautiful flowers went **(2)** _____ the car. Now he drives his green "garden car" to work every day.

The car is unusual, Moss **(3)** _____. "But I love driving it!" he says. "People look at me **(4)** _____ surprised, with their mouths open. Then they get big smiles on their faces. It's nice to see people happy!"

Moss's car changes every day because the plants grow**. Small, **(5)** _____ plants grow bigger. How do they stay alive? There are big bottles of water in the back of the car, and a hose*** keeps the plants wet.

And what is the best thing about the car? It **(6)** _____ so good!

_____

*chicken wire: metal netting
**grow: get bigger
***hose: a long, soft tube that brings water to the garden

Talk about the stories

Imagine that you and a partner are Kyrre Johansen and Keith Moss. You are meeting for the first time. Tell each other about your unusual cars.

12

Kind Woman Is a Winner

1. Read the story

Look at the pictures on these pages.
What is the story about? Now read it.

HAMPTON, VA., USA **¹**Twenty years ago, Mitzi Nichols, now 44, had a job at a hospital. Many sick people there needed a new kidney*. "Someday I want to **give away** one of my kidneys," she **decided** then. **²**In 2001, Nichols gave the **gift** of a kidney to Calvin Saunders. It was dangerous and **difficult**, and she did not know the man, but she **saved** his life.

³In 2004, Nichols **won** $500,000 in the Virginia lottery**. **⁴**She **bought** her first house and a **truck** for her husband. She gave her daughter money for **school**. **⁵**The happy **winner** also gave money to Calvin Saunders. "She's so kind," he says. "First she gave me the kidney, and now this."

⁶"When you do good things for people, good things will happen to you," **explains** Nichols.

---

*kidney: one of two parts inside your body; it has the shape of a bean
**lottery: a game where you buy a ticket and hope to get lucky

NEW WORDS

give away *v*	gift *n*	save *v*	buy *v*	school *n*	explain *v*
decide *v*	difficult *adj*	win *v*	truck *n*	winner *n*	

>> See Glossary on page 93. >>

2. Rate the story

How much did you like it? Mark an ✗.

Not at All   A Lot
①   ②   ③   ④   ⑤

3. Check your comprehension

Put the sentences in the correct order. Number them 1–6.

a. ____ She bought a house and gave some money to Saunders.

b. ____ Mitzi Nichols worked in a hospital and saw many sick people.

c. ____ Twenty years later, she gave away a kidney to Calvin Saunders.

d. ____ She won $500,000.

e. ____ She bought a ticket in the Virginia lottery.

f. ____ She decided to help a sick person someday.

4. Check your vocabulary

Complete the sentences with the New Words.

a. Nichols de_ _ _ed to give _ _ _ _ one of her kidneys.

b. She gave a g_ _ _ to Calvin Saunders and s_ _ _d his life.

c. After she _ _ _ the lottery, Nichols bou_ _ _ a tr_ _ _ for her husband.

d. "When you do good things for people," ex_ _ _ _ _s Nichols, "good things will happen to you."

5. Listen to the story ⊙ track 24

Now listen to the story two or three times. Look at the pictures below as you listen.

6. Retell the story

Cover the story and look at the pictures above. Retell the story using the New Words.

7. Answer the questions

About the story...

a. What did Nichols do for Calvin Saunders?

b. When did she first decide to do this?

c. What did Nichols win? How does she explain it?

d. How did she use her money?

About you...

e. What question would you like to ask Nichols?

f. What difficult thing will you do when you are older?

g. Would you like to win the lottery? Why or why not?

h. What did you buy last week?

8. Learn word partnerships

Study the partnerships below. Complete the sentences so they are true for you.

GIFT		
give get buy	a gift	**Nichols gave a gift to Calvin Saunders.** *I got a gift from my sister yesterday.* *Ya-ping bought a gift for you.*
a birthday a special an expensive	gift	*We're giving Kazu a birthday gift.* *Jon received a special gift last week.* *It's a very expensive gift.*

a. I _____ a birthday gift from _____.

b. I bought _____ gift for _____.

c. _____ gave _____ gift _____.

9. Learn word groups

Complete the sentences so they are true for you. Use words from the picture.

AT SCHOOL

a. Students at my school usually sit at _____.

b. My teacher often writes on _____.

c. We have _____ at the end of the year.

10. Take a dictation ● track 25

Use your own paper to write the dictation. Check your answers on page 87.

11. Complete the story

Use the words from the box to complete the story.

> bought   school   decided   explained   gave a special gift   exam

Kind People on Train Help Teenager

TOKYO, JAPAN   A Japanese train with thousands of passengers **(1)** _____ to a worried teenager.

The 15-year-old girl was on her way to an important **(2)** _____ at a **(3)** _____ near Tokyo. She **(4)** _____ a train ticket and then got on the wrong train. The train went straight into the middle of Tokyo without any other stops.

Surprised and worried, the girl **(5)** _____ her problem to some kind strangers near her. They found a train official* and told him about the girl's exam. "We'll make a special stop," the official quickly **(6)** _____, and the girl arrived at her 9:20 A.M. exam on time.

Later, the girl's family called the train official and thanked him. "It was just natural**," he said. "It was for her future***."

_____

* official: someone who does important work
** natural: normal or usual
*** future: the time that will come

 Talk about the stories

How are the stories of Calvin Saunders and the teenage girl similar? How are they different?

1. Match the words with the pictures.

____ **a.** elevator   ____ **d.** wind

____ **b.** tourist   ____ **e.** winner

____ **c.** engine   ____ **f.** gift

1.

2.
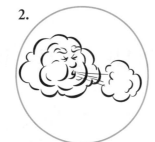

3.

4.

5.

6.

2. Write the words in the picture.

food   newspaper   eggs   plant   floor   refrigerator   bird

3. Are the sentences true or false? Check (✓) the correct box.

                                                                               T   F

a. Earthquakes can damage buildings.   ☐ ☐

b. Trucks and cars use gas.   ☐ ☐

c. Purple is a color between yellow and orange.   ☐ ☐

d. Windows have glass in them.   ☐ ☐

e. A plant is a person.   ☐ ☐

f. Both fish and birds can fly.   ☐ ☐

4. Circle the item that completes each sentence.

a. The book is _____ the TV.

   1. anywhere   2. on top of   3. inside   4. high

b. Did you _____ a fish?

   1. climb   2. jump   3. win   4. catch

c. There were only five _____ people at the party.

   1. other   2. alone   3. also   4. above

d. She _____ a lot of her money.

   1. hangs   2. gives away   3. decides   4. dries

e. The wind is so _____! It's hard to walk.

   1. modern   2. lucky   3. straight   4. strong

5. Match the words with the definitions.

a. strange ____   1. to tell someone about something to help the person understand it

b. smell ____   2. something that makes you worried

c. explain ____   3. very unusual or surprising

d. modern ____   4. not high

e. by ____   5. to notice something with your nose

f. problem ____   6. very new; not old

g. flat ____   7. not later than

6. Use the words from the box to complete the sentences.

glass	plant	saved	way	keeps	gave away
engine	reaches	dries	inside	tastes	just

a. Gel _____ Lexie Osburn's hair straight. When it _____, her hair stands tall.

b. It's wonderful to fly without an _____, says Felix Baumgartner. "It's _____ you, the sky, and your wings."

c. For 32 days, Kanchana Ketkeaw lived _____ a big _____ box with scorpions.

d. Tapei 101 is like a _____. It _____ to the sky.

e. Kyrre Johansen doesn't cook the _____ other people do, but his meat _____ good.

f. Mitzi Nichols _____ her kidney and _____ a man's life.

7. Use the words from the box to complete the story.

floor	on top of	saves	food
short	climb	kind	

Cats Everywhere

AKRON, OHIO, USA Linda Gilliland is never alone. She lives in a big house with her husband, Bob, and 150 cats! There are cats everywhere. They jump **(1)** _____ the chairs, **(2)** _____ up across the tables, and play on the **(3)** _____. There are white cats, black cats, cats with long hair, and cats with **(4)** _____ hair. Gilliland remembers all their names.

When people do not want their cats, Gilliland takes them into her home and **(5)** _____ their lives. Of course, 150 cats are a lot of work. Gilliland's many

(6) _____ friends help her. They come to the house and wash her floors. They bring

(7) _____ for the cats and play with them.

Gilliland's husband, a doctor, didn't always like cats. But now, he says, they are like his children.

8. Check (✓) *yes* or *no*.

Yes No

a. I have a work of art. ☐ ☐
b. I often win at sports. ☐ ☐
c. English is difficult for me. ☐ ☐
d. I want to buy a truck. ☐ ☐
e. There's an elevator in my school. ☐ ☐

Yes No

f. There are many tourists in my town. ☐ ☐
g. I usually save my money. ☐ ☐
h. I have a refrigerator in my kitchen. ☐ ☐
i. It's windy today in my town. ☐ ☐

9. Complete the sentences so they are true for you.

a. I often buy _____.
b. _____ is always kind to me.
c. The most popular newspaper in my town is _____.
d. I usually agree with _____.
e. My favorite food is _____.
f. I use my/a _____ every day.
g. I damaged my _____.
h. I'm so _____ today!

10. Fill in the chart with names of classmates. Try to write a different name in each blank. Walk around the room and ask questions such as:

Do you often play a sport?
Did you get a gift last week?

The winner is the first person to fill in seven blanks.

FIND SOMEONE WHO...

a. often plays a sport.
b. got a gift last week.
c. has a bird or a fish.
d. lives on the first or second floor.
e. would like to be an artist.
f. likes being a tourist.
g. has his/her own phone.
h. wants to open a business.
i. takes an elevator every day.
j. loves to cook.

13

Students Study with Animals

1. Read the story

Look at the pictures on these pages.
What is the story about? Now read it.

STANFORD, N.Y., USA   ¹Would you like to go to school with red **wolves**, pythons*, and emus**? ²The students at Millbrook School do. They **study** with 150 **wild** animals. **During** students' **lessons**, the red wolves cry. Big birds walk by the windows.

³Millbrook's teenagers live at the school. They have the usual lessons like English, writing, and **music**. ⁴But they also work at the school's **zoo**. They wash the animals and keep the zoo **clean**. They give the animals food—meat, eggs, fish, **fruit**, and **leaves**.

⁵Students at Millbrook learn a lot about plants and animals. The school teaches love for all things. ⁶Many teenagers in the modern world are bored and **careless**, says a teacher at the school. "But our teenagers learn to be **responsible**. The animals teach them that."

---

*pythons: big, dangerous snakes
**emus: tall birds that cannot fly

NEW WORDS

wolf *n*	during *prep*	zoo *n*	leaf *n*
study *v*	lesson *n*	clean *adj*	careless *adj*
wild *adj*	music *n*	fruit *n*	responsible *adj*

>> See Glossary on page 94. >>

2. Rate the story

How much did you like it? Mark an ✗.

Not at All   A Lot
① ② ③ ④ ⑤

3. Check your comprehension

Check (✔) the endings that are true.

a. Students at Millbrook

___ work at a zoo.

___ live at home.

___ are bored and careless.

___ learn to love animals.

b. The animals

___ eat things like fish and fruit.

___ have music lessons.

___ keep the zoo clean.

___ teach the students a lot.

4. Check your vocabulary

Complete the sentences with the New Words.

a. Students at Millbrook study with w_ _ _ animals like red w_ _ _es.

b. They work at the school's z_ _ and keep the animals cl_ _ _.

c. They give the animals fr_ _ _, eggs, fish, and l_ _ves.

d. Millbrook's students are not bored or care_ _ _ _.

5. Listen to the story   track 26

Now listen to the story two or three times. Look at the pictures below as you listen.

6. Retell the story

Cover the story and look at the pictures above. Retell the story using the New Words.

7. Answer the questions

About the story…

a. What is unusual about Millbrook School?

b. What happens during lessons?

c. What foods do students give the animals?

d. Why does the school have a zoo?

About you…

e. Would you like to study at Millbrook School? Why or why not?

f. Do you like to go to the zoo? What animals do you like to see at the zoo?

g. Do you have an animal? What does the animal teach you?

h. Are you a responsible person? How?

8. Learn word partnerships

Study the partnerships below. Complete the sentences so they are true for you.

STUDY		
study	with something	**The students study with 150 animals.**
	with someone	*I'm studying with 30 classmates.*
	something	*We study music, math, and English.*
	hard	*Megumi always studies hard.*
	for an exam	*Jae-won studied for his exam last week.*

a. I study _____ almost every day.

b. I studied _____ last week.

c. I _____ with _____.

9. Learn word groups

Complete the sentences so they are true for you. Use words from the pictures.

FOOD GROUPS

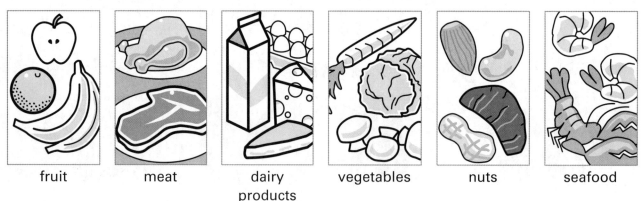

fruit   meat   dairy products   vegetables   nuts   seafood

a. I eat a lot of _____ and _____.

b. I don't often eat _____.

c. Yesterday I ate some _____, _____, and _____.

10. Take a dictation track 27

Use your own paper to write the dictation. Check your answers on page 87.

11. Complete the story

Use the words from the box to complete the story.

studies with	wild	during	lessons	music	responsible

Cat Studies with Students

SOQUEL, CALIF., USA Every morning, Bobby is the first to arrive at the elementary school* in Soquel. He is never late for school.

Bobby is a **(1)** _____ but unusual student—he's a cat! He lives near the school with the Brown family. Two years ago, he began following young Laura Brown to her **(2)** _____. When Laura went from the second to the third grade**, Bobby stayed in the second grade with his favorite teacher, Pam Aguilar.

Now Bobby walks to school by himself every morning. He waits for his teacher at the door. **(3)** _____ lessons, he **(4)** _____ the children. He sits on their books when they read. He sleeps in the teacher's chair when she plays

(5) _____. After school, he plays with **(6)** _____ cats.

Bobby teaches students about animals. "We like having him in school," says Aguilar. "He makes us laugh." _____

* elementary school: a school for young children
** grade: a class in school that lasts for a year

Talk about the stories

How are the schools in the two stories similar? How are they different?

14

A Wild Ride

1. Read the story

Look at the pictures on these pages.
What is the story about? Now read it.

HASSLOCH, GERMANY [1]For 192 hours in 2003, Richard Rodriguez **went around** and around, up and down. His heart was often in his throat*. [2]When he finished the **wild** roller coaster** **ride**, this English teacher from Chicago was tired and **confused**, but **really** happy. It was the longest roller coaster ride **ever**!

[3]Rodriguez slept while he rode the German roller coaster. The **seats** in his little car were very soft, but it was not easy. The first night he slept only an hour. "Your body learns to sleep after **a few** days," explained Rodriguez. [4]His car also had a little **toilet**. [5]Every eight hours, he stopped for a short 15-minute **rest**. [6]The biggest problem was the hot August sun. Rodriguez had a lot of water with him. He drank most of it and put **the rest** on his head.

---

* his heart was in his throat: he felt afraid
** roller coaster: an exciting train in an amusement park

NEW WORDS

go around v	**ride** n	**really** adv	**seat** n	**toilet** n	**the rest** n
wild adj	**confused** adj	**ever** adv	**a few** det	**rest** n	

>> See Glossary on page 94. >>

2. Rate the story

How much did you like it? Mark an ✗.

Not at All   A Lot
①   ②   ③   ④   ⑤

3. Check your comprehension

Correct five mistakes in the story summary.

Rodriguez went around and around on a roller coaster for 92 hours. When he finished the wild ride, he was confused and really sad. It was not hard for him to sleep while he rode. Every two hours, he stopped for a rest. The biggest problem was the rain.

4. Check your vocabulary

Complete the sentences with the New Words.

a. Rodriguez's ride was rea_ _ _ long and very wi_ _.

b. After he went ar_ _ _ _ for 192 hours, he got very con_ _ _ _ _.

c. His roller coaster car had soft s_ _ _s and a to_ _ _ _.

d. Rodriguez put the r_ _ _ of his water on his head.

5. Listen to the story   track 28

Now listen to the story two or three times. Look at the pictures below as you listen.

6. Retell the story

Cover the story and look at the pictures above. Retell the story using the New Words.

7. Answer the questions

About the story...

a. How did Rodriguez feel when he finished his 192-hour ride?

b. What was unusual about his roller coaster car?

c. What was his biggest problem during the ride?

d. What does Rodriguez do when he isn't riding roller coasters?

About you...

e. What question would you like to ask Rodriguez?

f. Do you like wild roller coasters? Why or why not?

g. What is the longest ride you ever had in a car, bus, train, or plane?

h. When do you feel confused? Tired? Happy?

8. Learn word partnerships

Study the partnerships below. Complete the sentences so they are true for you.

A REST		
stop for take have need	a rest	***Rodriguez stopped for a rest.*** *Ya-ping likes to take a rest after school.* *I usually have a rest before dinner.* *Do you need a rest?*
a 10- (15-, 20-, 30-) minute a long/short	rest	*Rodriguez stopped for a 15-minute rest.* *Sumio took a long rest yesterday.*

a. Last weekend, I took _____ rest.

b. I often _____ a rest after _____.

c. I'll have _____ rest _____.

9. Learn word groups

Complete the sentences so they are true. Use words from the pictures.

DIRECTIONS

  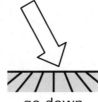

go around   go through   go under   go down   go up   go over

a. Some roller coasters _____ water, and you get wet.

b. When you fly from Asia to California, you _____ the Pacific.

c. To get to the 91st floor of Taipei 101, you _____ in the elevator.

d. When you are on the river Thames, you _____ London Bridge.

10. Take a dictation track 29

Use your own paper to write the dictation. Check your answers on page 87.

11. Complete the story

Use the words from the box to complete the story.

| confused | ride | ever | a few | wild | around | went up | seats |

Wig Stops Roller Coaster

NEW YORK CITY, USA   People were having fun on a **(1)** _____ New York City roller coaster in 2004 when it suddenly stopped–23 meters up in the air! For 30 minutes, the riders sat in their **(2)** _____ and waited. They were **(3)** _____. "Why are workers climbing over the tracks*?" they asked.

"We're looking for the problem!" a worker cried. And they were surprised when they found it. A woman's dark brown wig** was in the wheels*** of the roller coaster. After they got the wig out, **(4)** _____ workers pushed the cars down the hill. The **(5)** _____ began again. The cars **(6)** _____ and down, over and **(7)** _____. There were no more problems.

Where did the wig come from? "We won't **(8)** _____ know," said a worker. "It flew off a woman's head and onto the tracks–maybe from the ride before."

_____

   * tracks: metal lines that a train runs on
  ** wig: hair that people wear that is not their own
 *** wheels: things like circles that turn around and around to move something

 Talk about the stories

Which story is more surprising? Which one did you like better? Why?

15

53½ Hot Dogs

1. Read the story

Look at the pictures on these pages.
What is the story about? Now read it.

NEW YORK CITY, USA **¹**Who can eat the most hot dogs* in 12 minutes? **Each** year on the July 4 **holiday**, Nathan's Famous restaurant in New York City has a contest** to **find out**. The best eaters in the world come to the restaurant. **²**Takeru "Tsunami" Kobayashi of Japan **entered** the contest in 2001, 2002, 2003, and 2004 and won all four times!

³Kobayashi, 26, is a **thin** man—**as** thin **as** a **pencil**. Many other eaters in the contest are much bigger **than** Kobayashi. **⁴**But **never mind**—Kobayashi can eat faster! At Nathan's, he pushes in two hot dogs at once. **⁵**He **dances** just **a little** while he eats. "It helps me," he explains. "I eat **even** faster when I dance." **⁶**In 2004, his best year ever, Kobayashi finished 53½ hot dogs in 12 minutes. "He's the best," say people at Nathan's. "**No one** ever ate so many."

*hot dogs: frankfurters (meat) inside bread
**contest: a game or test that people try to win

NEW WORDS

each *det*	**enter** *v*	**pencil** *n*	**dance** *v*	**no one** *pron*
holiday *n*	**thin** *adj*	**than** *conj*	**a little** *adv*	
find out *v*	**as...as** *conj*	**never mind** *interj*	**even** *adv*	

>> See Glossary on page 95. >>

2. Rate the story

How much did you like it? Mark an ✗.

Not at All   A Lot
① ② ③ ④ ⑤

3. Check your comprehension

Match the first and second parts of the sentences.

a. Nathan's restaurant has ___
b. Some eaters are ___
c. Kobayashi is ___
d. He can eat ___
e. He dances ___
f. He finished ___

1. a thin man but a big eater.
2. two hot dogs at the same time.
3. first in 2004.
4. a hot dog contest.
5. very big.
6. when he eats.

4. Check your vocabulary

Complete the sentences with the New Words.

a. Who can eat the most hot dogs? Nathan's has a contest e_ _ _ year to find _ _ _.
b. Kobayashi is as thin _ _ a pen_ _ _, but he e_ _ _ _ed and won the contest four times.
c. Kobayashi eats fast. He can eat e_ _ _ faster when he d_ _ _es a lit_ _ _.
d. Before Kobayashi, no _ _ _ ever ate 53½ hot dogs in 12 minutes.

5. Listen to the story   track 30

Now listen to the story two or three times. Look at the pictures below as you listen.

6. Retell the story

Cover the story and look at the pictures above. Retell the story using the New Words.

7. Answer the questions

About the story…

a. Why is Kobayashi famous?

b. How big is he? How big are the other eaters?

c. What does Kobayashi do while he eats? Why?

d. What was his best year ever? How many hot dogs did he finish?

About you…

e. Would you like to enter Nathan's contest? Why or why not?

f. What is your favorite food? How much can you eat?

g. Do you ever enter contests? What kind?

h. What is your favorite holiday? What do you do?

8. Learn word partnerships

Study the partnerships below. Complete the sentences so they are true for you.

AS…AS	
as thin as a pencil	**Kobayashi is as thin as a pencil.**
as busy as a bee	*She never stops working; she's as busy as a bee.*
as sick as a dog	*I was as sick as a dog last week.*
as good as gold	*Your baby never cries; he's as good as gold!*
as old as the hills	*My computer is as old as the hills.*

a. My _____ is _____ the hills.

b. _____ as gold.

c. I am as _____ as _____ .

9. Learn word groups

Complete the sentences so they are true for you. Use words from the pictures.

DESCRIBING PEOPLE

fat   thin   tall   short   strong   weak

a. I am not _____ or _____ .

b. When I was a child, I was _____ and _____ .

c. My good friend is very _____ .

10. Take a dictation track 31

Use your own paper to write the dictation. Check your answers on page 87.

11. Complete the story

Use the words from the box to complete the story.

tall	even	never mind	each	than	fat	holidays

Man Eats 18 Cows

FOND DU LAC, WISC., USA **(1)** _____ day, Donald Gorske, 50, eats two or three big hamburgers with cheese*. From 1972 to 2005, he ate more **(2)** _____ 20,000 Big Mac sandwiches from McDonald's restaurant. That's almost 18 cows** and hundreds of kilograms of cheese!

  Gorske's wife, Mary, never cooks meals for him. But **(3)** _____–Gorske likes it that way! He **(4)** _____ likes hamburgers more than meals at home. He does not like eating any other food like eggs, fish, or fruit. On **(5)** _____ like Christmas, he eats only Big Macs. Gorske always keeps a lot of hamburgers in his refrigerator.

  The man is really **(6)** _____–about 1.83 meters–but not **(7)** _____. He almost never gets sick. "I love hamburgers," he says. "Why stop eating them?"

---

  * cheese: yellow or white food made from milk
 ** cows: big farm animals that give milk

 Talk about the stories

Imagine that you and a partner are Takeru Kobayashi and Donald Gorske. You are meeting for the first time. Tell each other about your unusual meals.

16

Man Leaves Wife in the Atlantic

1. Read the story

Look at the pictures on these pages. What is the story about? Now read it.

LONDON, ENGLAND ¹Debra Veal and her husband, Andrew, pushed their small **boat** into the water from an **island** near Africa. ²Then they began to **row** 4,700 kilometers across the Atlantic. They were in a **race** with 35 other rowboats*.

³After two weeks, Andrew suddenly got **scared**. He could not eat or sleep. "I can't **go on**," he told his wife. They called for help, and a boat came for him.

⁴The British woman finished the race by herself. She was often **in danger**. She rowed for 111 days, alone with **storms**, huge **waves**, and sharks**. Once a **large** ship nearly hit her. ⁵She was **lonely**, too, but she really **enjoyed** the adventure. ⁶Debra **finally** arrived in Barbados. She did not win, but she **was proud of** herself and happy to see Andrew. "It's OK for men to be afraid," she said. "I'm proud of him, too."

---

*rowboats: small boats with no engines
**sharks: big fish with sharp teeth that live in the sea

NEW WORDS

boat *n*	race *n*	in danger *adv*	large *adj*	finally *adv*
island *n*	scared *adj*	storm *n*	lonely *adj*	be proud of *v*
row *v*	go on *v*	wave *n*	enjoy *v*	

>> See Glossary on page 95. >>

2. Rate the story

How much did you like it? Mark an ✗.

Not at All   A Lot
1   2   3   4   5

3. Check your comprehension

Put the sentences in the correct order. Number them 1–6.

a. ___ Andrew called for help because he was scared.

b. ___ Debra decided to go on alone.

c. ___ They began to row across the Atlantic.

d. ___ Debra and her husband left from an island near Africa.

e. ___ Debra finally got to Barbados.

f. ___ She was often in danger from ships, storms, and sharks.

4. Check your vocabulary

Complete the sentences with the New Words.

a. After two weeks in the r_ _ _, Andrew could not go _ _.

b. Debra r_ _ed the boat by herself, and she was often lon_ _ _.

c. Once a la_ _ _ ship almost hit her, and there were big st_ _ _s.

d. When Debra fin_ _ _ _ arrived in Barbados, she was pr_ _ _ of herself.

5. Listen to the story track 32

Now listen to the story two or three times. Look at the pictures below as you listen.

6. Retell the story

Cover the story and look at the pictures above. Retell the story using the New Words.

7. Answer the questions

About the story...

a. Where did the race begin and finish?

b. What do you think? Why did Andrew get scared?

c. Why was Debra in danger?

d. How does she feel about her husband now?

About you...

e. What do you think of Debra?

f. What question would you like to ask her?

g. Were you ever in danger? What happened?

h. What do you enjoy about the sea?

8. Learn word partnerships

Study the partnerships below. Complete the sentences so they are true for you.

ENJOY		
(really) enjoy	something	***Debra really enjoyed the adventure.***
		I enjoy movies and television.
		We really enjoy baseball and soccer.
	doing something	*I don't enjoy swimming.*
		Naoko really enjoyed meeting you.
		My family enjoys cooking on weekends.

a. I enjoyed _____ when I was a child.

b. My family _____ enjoys _____.

c. I don't enjoy _____.

9. Learn word groups

Complete the sentences so they are true for you. Use words from the pictures.

BOATS

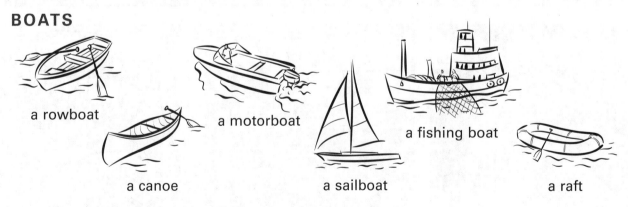

a rowboat   a motorboat   a fishing boat

a canoe   a sailboat   a raft

a. I would like to ride in _____.

b. I would not like to ride in _____.

c. When I was younger, I rode in _____.

10. Take a dictation track 33

Use your own paper to write the dictation. Check your answers on page 87.

11. Complete the story

Use the words from the box to complete the story.

| waves | enjoying | scared | motorboat | large | island |

Friends Fly into Lake

KENORA, ONTARIO, CANADA   Five Canadian friends were riding in a **(1)** _____ on a lake* in Ontario. It was summer, and everyone was **(2)** _____ the day. The driver was going fast over the **(3)** _____ when someone opened a **(4)** _____ box of food. Out flew a plastic** bag. It hit the driver's face and stayed there because the wind was so strong. He could not take it off his head, and he could not see a thing.

   The boat was still moving fast when it hit a small **(5)** _____ in the middle of the lake. All five friends flew out of the boat and into the water. They were surprised and **(6)** _____! But nobody got hurt***, and everyone swam to the island.

   * lake: a big area of water, smaller than a sea
  ** plastic: a strong but light material
*** hurt: injured

Talk about the stories

Imagine that you and a partner are Debra Veal and the driver of the motorboat. You are meeting for the first time. Tell each other about your boat adventures.

17

Leopard Man

1. Read the story

Look at the pictures on these pages. What is the story about? Now read it.

ISLE OF SKYE, SCOTLAND **¹**Tom Leppard, 68, has tattoos* from head to foot—the most tattoos in the world. They make him look like a leopard**. **²**Tom lives alone on an island. He moved there 15 years ago and **built** a house with **sticks**, trees, and large **stones**. It has no water, **heat**, or **lights**. **³**Tom takes a bath in the river near his house and **fishes** there, too. He is never **in a hurry**.

⁴Once a week, he puts on his clothes, gets into his small boat, and rows to town. He buys food and books. He loves to read about the **history** of the world.

⁵The winter is hard for him because this **corner** of Scotland is cold. **⁶**But Tom is happy to **escape** the modern world. "I like **life** here. I do **not** need **anything** more. I'm lonely in town, but I'm never lonely here."

*tattoos: pictures on someone's skin
**leopard: a wild animal, like a big cat, that is yellow with black circles

NEW WORDS

build *v*	**heat** *n*	**in a hurry** *adj*	**escape** *v*
stick *n*	**light** *n*	**history** *n*	**life** *n*
stone *n*	**fish** *v*	**corner** *n*	**not…anything** *pron*

>> See Glossary on page 96. >>

2. Rate the story

How much did you like it? Mark an ✗.

Not at All   A Lot
① ② ③ ④ ⑤

3. Check your comprehension

Check (✔) the endings that are true.

a. Tom Leppard is

___ a young man.

___ often in a hurry.

___ a reader.

___ a leopard.

b. He likes

___ tattoos.

___ history.

___ modern life.

___ his island.

4. Check your vocabulary

Complete the sentences with the New Words.

a. Tom built his home with large sto_ _s, trees, and sti_ _s.

b. He likes to f_ _ _ in the river near his home and is never in a h_ _ _ _.

c. He enjoys reading hi_ _ _ _ _ books.

d. He likes his l_ _ _, and he says, "I don't need an_ _ _ _ _ _ more."

5. Listen to the story ⊙ track 34

Now listen to the story two or three times. Look at the pictures below as you listen.

6. Retell the story

Cover the story and look at the pictures above. Retell the story using the New Words.

7. Answer the questions

About the story…

a. What is special about Tom?

b. What kind of house did he build?

c. How does he get food?

d. What does he want to escape? Why?

About you…

e. What question would you like to ask Tom?

f. Would you like to live like him? Why or why not?

g. What do you do when you are lonely?

h. What do you think? Are people in the modern world too often in a hurry?

8. Learn word partnerships

Study the partnerships below. Complete the sentences so they are true for you.

BUILD		
build	a house / a home	**Tom built a house with stones and trees.**
	an airport	*Seoul built an airport in 2001.*
	a school	*My town is going to build a new school.*
	a shopping mall	*The city will build a shopping mall.*
	a stadium	*I want my town to build a new stadium.*
	a skyscraper	*Taipei built the tallest skyscraper.*

a. My town built a new _____.

b. I want my town to build _____.

c. _____ built _____.

9. Learn word groups

Complete the sentences so they are true for you. Use words from the picture.

RIVER ACTIVITIES

a. When I was a child, I liked to _____ in the river.

b. I didn't _____ there.

c. Someday I would like to _____ in a big river.

10. Take a dictation track 35

Use your own paper to write the dictation. Check your answers on page 87.

11. Complete the story

Use the words from the box to complete the story.

| lights | in a hurry | corner | escape | build a house | heat | life |

Woman Builds Her Own Home

FAIRBANKS, ALASKA, USA Jeannine Patane always wanted to **(1)** _____ in Alaska. For two years, she lived in her car and saved her money. And then, for the next three years, she looked everywhere for some beautiful land* for her house. She wanted to **(2)** _____ the modern world. Finally, she found some land in the woods** and began her work.

She built her house all by herself. It is small—about four meters by four meters. She has **(3)** _____ because winters in this **(4)** _____ of the world are cold. And there are **(5)** _____ because the winters are dark. The house has no water. Patane brings water from town and takes a bath with rainwater or snow***.

(6) _____ in Alaska is slow, and Patane is never **(7)** _____. "I love summers," she says. "I go out and just listen. I watch the birds and the animals."
_____

* land: a piece of ground
** woods: a place with many trees
*** snow: soft, white stuff that falls from the sky when it is cold

Talk about the stories

How are the lives of Tom Leppard and Jeannine Patane similar? How are they different? Which home would you most like to visit?

18

Making an International Star

1. Read the story

Look at the pictures on these pages.
What is the story about? Now read it.

KOREA **1**At 13, the Korean pop singer BoA made her first CD. It was **immediately** popular. In 2004, four years later, she won MTV's "Most **Influential** Asian Artist" award*.

2How did BoA **become** a **star** so fast? The people at a Korean recording studio** wanted a **future** girl star. They looked everywhere. When BoA's older brother went to the studio and sang for them, they asked, "Do you have a younger sister?"

3The answer to their question was BoA. She was only 11, but she sang and danced beautifully. The people at the studio were excited and quickly told her **parents** about their **plan**. **4**BoA's parents **were against** it. They wanted their daughter to study, not sing. But **at last** they agreed.

5The studio immediately gave BoA Japanese and English lessons. (An **international** star needs languages!) Later she got dance and music lessons. **6**Now BoA performs for huge **crowds** in Asia and is ready to conquer*** the world.

---

   * award: something that you win for very good work
  ** recording studio: a place that makes music
*** conquer: to win something by fighting for it

NEW WORDS

immediately *adv*	**become** *v*	**future** *adj*	**plan** *n*	**at last** *adv*	**crowd** *n*
influential *adj*	**star** *n*	**parent** *n*	**be against** *v*	**international** *adj*	

>> See Glossary on page 96. >>

2. Rate the story

How much did you like it? Mark an **✗**.

Not at All   A Lot

1   2   3   4   5

3. Check your comprehension

Put the sentences in the correct order. Number them 1–6.

a. ___ BoA made her first CD.

b. ___ Now the star performs for crowds in Asia.

c. ___ Her parents said OK to the recording studio's plan.

d. ___ BoA got lessons in English and Japanese.

e. ___ The people at the studio were excited about BoA.

f. ___ BoA's brother told the recording studio about his younger sister.

4. Check your vocabulary

Complete the sentences with the New Words.

a. BoA is an influ_ _ _ _ _ _ Asian pop st_ _.

b. She wanted to bec_ _ _ a singer at 11, but her mother and father were aga_ _ _ _ it.

c. But BoA's par_ _ _s agreed at l_ _ _.

d. Now BoA is an inter_ _ _ _ _ _ _ _ star and performs for big c_ _ _ _s in Asia.

5. Listen to the story   track 36

Now listen to the story two or three times. Look at the pictures below as you listen.

6. Retell the story

Cover the story and look at the pictures above. Retell the story using the New Words.

7. Answer the questions

About the story…

a. What did BoA win in 2004?

b. Who made her a star?

c. How did her parents feel about the recording studio's plan?

d. Who does BoA perform for?

About you…

e. What question would you like to ask BoA?

f. Would you like to become a star? Why or why not?

g. Which music or sports stars are influential in your country?

h. What plans do you have for your future?

8. Learn word partnerships

Study the partnerships below. Complete the sentences so they are true for you.

INTERNATIONAL		
an international	star	**BoA is an international pop star.**
	language	*English is an international language.*
	problem	*Pollution is an international problem.*
	flight	*I'm taking an international flight to Istanbul.*
	(soccer) match	*We played in an international match.*
	organization	*The UN is an international organization.*

a. I really like the international star _____.

b. I would like to take an international _____ to _____.

c. _____ is an _____ problem. We need to work on it together!

9. Learn word groups

Complete the sentences so they are true. Use words from the pictures.

STARS

a singer   an actor   an athlete   a dancer   a musician

a. Jackie Chan is _____, and Leonardo DiCaprio and Nicole Kidman are, too.

b. Tiger Woods is _____, and Ichiro Suzuki and Yao Ming are, too.

c. I would like to be _____ but not _____.

10. Take a dictation track 37

Use your own paper to write the dictation. Check your answers on page 87.

11. Complete the story

Use the words from the box to complete the story.

| become | star | plans | parents | international | crowds |

Becoming a World-Famous Violinist

"but I'm still learning—about music and about life."

PHILADELPHIA, USA   When she was just three years old, Sarah Chang asked her **(1)** _____ for a violin*. At eight, the little girl began to perform with the best orchestras** in New York City and Philadelphia. She made her first CD at nine. Sarah is a **(2)** _____–one of the best violinists*** ever. She plays her violin for **(3)** _____ in many countries in the world.

How did Sarah, now 23, **(4)** _____ an **(5)** _____ star? She worked a lot when she was a child and a teenager. She played her violin for three hours every day after school. "Really, I was never interested in anything but music," she explains.

Born in Philadelphia to Korean parents, Sarah had a lot of help with her future **(6)** _____. Her father was her first violin teacher, and her mother writes and plays music. Her recording studio helped her, too. "I love to perform," says Sarah,

  * violin: a musical instrument made of wood, with strings
 ** orchestras: big groups of people who play different musical instruments together
*** violinists: people who play the violin

 Talk about the stories

Imagine that you and a partner are BoA and Sarah Chang. You are meeting for the first time. Tell each other about your lives.

1. Match the words with the pictures.

___ **a.** wolf
___ **b.** light
___ **c.** toilet

___ **d.** stick
___ **e.** pencil
___ **f.** seat

1.

2.

3.
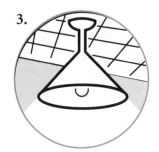

4.

5.

6.

2. Write the words in the picture.

| storm | boat | island | wave | crowd | leaf |

3. Are the sentences true or false? Check (✓) the correct box.

		T	F
a.	A wolf is a wild animal.	☐	☐
b.	When you enjoy something, you like it.	☐	☐
c.	Your parents are as young as you are.	☐	☐
d.	A stone is a fruit.	☐	☐
e.	A tree is larger than a leaf.	☐	☐
f.	The world goes around the sun.	☐	☐

4. Circle the item that completes each sentence.

a. Let's watch _____ the movie!

    1. at last   2. the rest of   3. never mind   4. ever

b. I'm _____ in a hurry.

    1. lonely   2. a few   3. really   4. immediately

c. Were you ever scared _____ the storm?

    1. a little   2. finally   3. in danger   4. during

d. I had a 30-minute _____, so I'm not tired now.

    1. rest   2. heat   3. corner   4. ride

e. Jill wants to become a singer, but her parents are _____ it.

    1. proud of   2. against   3. escaping   4. entering

5. Match the words with the definitions.

a. heat ___	1. to learn something that you did not know before
b. light ___	2. after a long time; finally
c. be proud of ___	3. feeling bad because you are alone
d. find out ___	4. to be pleased about something that you or others do or did
e. lonely ___	5. something that makes a place warm
f. in danger ___	6. in a bad situation
g. at last ___	7. some, but not much
h. a little ___	8. something that helps people see in the dark

6. Use the words from the box to complete the sentences.

scared	careless	influential	pencil	life	go on
immediately	went around	thin	responsible	anything	wild

a. The students at Millbrook School aren't bored or _____; they learn to be _____.

b. Richard Rodriguez _____ for 192 hours on a _____ roller coaster ride.

c. Takeru Kobayashi isn't a large man; he's as _____ as a _____.

d. When Debra Veal's husband got _____ in the Atlantic, he told her, "I can't _____."

e. Tom Leppard likes _____ on his island. He says, "I don't need _____ more."

f. BoA's first CD was _____ popular, and then she won the "Most _____ Asian Artist" award.

7. Use the words from the box to complete the story.

	than	each	as	
future	finally	clean	even	

Taller and Taller

THE NETHERLANDS The Dutch are the tallest people in the world, and they are getting taller every day. Forty years ago, the average* Dutch man was 170 centimeters tall. Today, he is 185 centimeters, ten centimeters taller **(1)** _____ the average American man. Why are the Dutch so tall? The Netherlands is a rich, **(2)** _____ country. Also, the Dutch eat good food and drink a lot of milk. And **(3)** _____, they have good doctors.

By 2025, the Dutch will get **(4)** _____ taller—maybe by ten centimeters. **(5)** _____ year people there ask for longer pants and larger shirts at the clothes stores.

But now the Dutch are beginning to eat a lot of junk food, like hamburgers and hot dogs. Will they go on doing this? Then, maybe, in **(6)** _____ years they will not be **(7)** _____ tall as they are today.

*average: what is usual or ordinary

8. Check (✓) *yes* or *no*.

		Yes	No			Yes	No
a.	I often go to the zoo.	☐	☐	e.	I like to study history.	☐	☐
b.	I'm a careless person.	☐	☐	f.	I really love to dance.	☐	☐
c.	I would like to become an international star.	☐	☐	g.	I like large crowds.	☐	☐
d.	I'm often in a hurry.	☐	☐	h.	I have many future plans.	☐	☐

9. Complete the sentences so they are true for you.

a. I have only a few _____.

b. I am as _____ as _____.

c. I would like to become _____.

d. I want to escape _____.

e. My favorite holiday is _____.

f. I do not enjoy _____.

g. I get scared when _____.

h. I'm more responsible than _____.

10. Fill in the chart with names of classmates. Try to write a different name in each blank. Walk around the room and ask questions such as:

Did you ever win a race?
Are you sometimes confused during lessons?

The winner is the first person to fill in seven blanks.

FIND SOMEONE WHO...

a. won a race.

b. is sometimes confused during lessons.

c. enjoys roller coasters.

d. wants to be a pop star.

e. would like to build a house.

f. is very happy with his or her life.

g. rowed a boat last summer.

h. loves to listen to music.

i. eats a lot of fruit.

j. has international friends.

Unit 1

When Scott went out for dinner, his nametag was still on his shirt. Strangers were very friendly and began conversations. Now Scott wears a nametag everywhere—at parks, shopping malls, and movie theaters. "Nametags make people comfortable," he says.

Unit 2

Oeun is a tiny boy, and his python is huge. When they sleep, Lucky makes a circle with his body. Oeun is in the middle. They are always together. Once the family took a short trip. Oeun missed Lucky, so the family came back early.

Unit 3

There is a great, new car from China. It costs a lot, but it has a karaoke machine. While you wait in busy traffic, you and your passengers can sing pop songs. Be careful! It can be dangerous when you drive and sing at the same time.

Unit 4

Children and teenagers love Mud Day. They push their friends into the soft, wet mud and have mud fights. They swim in the mud. Then fire fighters wash them with their hoses, and the kids go home and take a bath.

Unit 5

People have to look at Rashid. His long mustache flies up into the air like two wings. Rashid is traveling to many countries, and his mustache is paying for the trip. It pays for his hotels and his lunches and dinners.

Unit 6

Neil left his job as a lawyer and followed his heart to South America. Now he is riding through ten countries by himself. He carries his tent, bed, and clothes on his bike. He performs for children and adults.

Unit 7

Lexie's hair is straight and spiky. She uses gel on it. This keeps it tall. Sometimes she puts colors like purple in her hair, and sometimes she cuts the sides. She likes her hair, but she has a problem with it when it is windy. It goes flat!

Unit 8

Felix flew above the English Channel like a bird. He had his own wings but no engine. His wings caught the wind, and he flew fast. A business will soon sell the suit with wings. Maybe this will be a popular and exciting sport some day.

Unit 9

Kanchana, an artist, lived inside a glass box for 32 days. She was alone, so she could only talk to scorpions. She gave them some delicious food. They climbed on her bed, up the walls, and over the wood floor. But Kanchana wasn't afraid.

Unit 10

Taipei 101 stands high above the other buildings in Taipei. With 101 floors, it reaches to the sky like a plant. The elevators are the most modern in the world. Taiwan's strong earthquakes will not damage the building.

Unit 11

Johansen does not cook in his kitchen. He makes fish and steak on top of his car engine. On short trips, he cooks hot dogs. He saves a lot of time this way. His meat does not smell like gas. It tastes so good!

Unit 12

Nichols gave away a kidney to Saunders. It was dangerous and difficult for her, but she saved his life. Later, she was a winner in the lottery. She bought a house and a truck for her husband. She also gave a new gift to Saunders.

Unit 13

During lessons at Millbrook School, the red wolves cry. Students at the school study music and English, but they also work with animals. They keep the zoo clean and give the wild animals vegetables, leaves, nuts, and fruit. Students at the school learn to be responsible, not careless.

Unit 14

Rodriguez went up, down, and around and around for 192 wild hours. His car had soft seats and a little toilet. During the long ride, he got confused and really tired. It was hot, so he drank a lot of water and put some on his head.

Unit 15

Kobayashi is as thin as a pencil, but never mind. He can eat a lot! He entered and won the contest at Nathan's four times. He dances a little while he eats. His best year ever was 2004. He ate 53½ hot dogs in 12 minutes.

Unit 16

When Debra's husband could not go on, she rowed the boat by herself. There were storms, large waves, and sharks. She was often lonely and in danger, but she really enjoyed the adventure. She was proud of herself when she finally arrived in Barbados.

Unit 17

Tom Leppard built his house with stones, sticks, and trees. He lives without heat or lights. He likes to fish and sunbathe in the river near his home, and he is never in a hurry. He enjoys his life and does not need anything more.

Unit 18

BoA is an influential singer and dancer. She performs for huge crowds in Asia. Her first CD was immediately popular, and she became an international pop star very fast. Her parents were against the studio's plan at first, but now they are proud of BoA.

Glossary

Unit 1

go out *v* to leave the place where you live or work

restaurant *n* you can eat there

still *adv* a word that shows that nothing changed

stranger *n* someone you do not know

friendly *adj* nice to people

conversation *n* when two or more people talk about something

everywhere *adv* in all places

park *n* an open place with trees and flowers; you can walk and play there

make *v* to cause something to happen

comfortable *adj* feeling happy and relaxed

silence *n* when there is silence, there is no noise

wall *n* something that keeps people apart; it is also a strong and hard thing between rooms or houses, or around a town

Unit 2

unusual *adj* not usual; you do not often see something that is unusual

huge *adj* very big

together *adv* with each other or near each other

circle *n* a round shape; "O" is a circle

middle *n* the part in the center

worried *adj* feeling that something bad can happen

special *adj* not usual; important

life *n* the time that you are alive

favorite *adj* someone or something that you like best

trip *n* a short journey to a place and back again

miss *v* to feel bad because you are not with someone or something

Unit 3

traffic *n* all the cars, etc., on the road

busy *adj* with a lot of things happening

bored *adj* not feeling happy because you have nothing interesting to do

while *conj* at the same time

line *n* things or people one after another

great *adj* very good; wonderful

machine *n* a thing with parts that move and do work

passenger *n* someone in a car who is not driving

pop song *n* music that a lot of young people like

will *v* a word that you use to show the future

cost *v* to have the price of

dangerous *adj* something that is dangerous can be bad for you

Unit 4

party *n* a meeting of friends where people eat, drink, talk, and laugh

dirt *n* black stuff from the ground

mud *n* dirt with water

teenager *n* someone who is between 13 and 19 years old

soft *adj* not hard; something soft moves when you put your hand on it

swim *v* to move your body through water

fight *n* when people fight, they hit others

fire fighter *n* someone who stops fires

wash *v* to clean someone or something with water

wet *adj* having water in or on someone or something

take a bath *v* to wash your body in a bathtub

push *v* to move someone or something away from you

fun *n* something that you like to do

Unit 5

surprised *adj* you feel surprised when you see or hear something unusual or different

have to *v* must

mustache *n* the hair between someone's mouth and nose

world *n* all the countries and their people

fly *v* to move through the air

air *n* the space around and over things

like *prep* in the same way as someone or something

wing *n* the part of a bird or airplane that helps it fly

travel *v* to go from one place to another

pay *v* to give money for something

adventure *n* something exciting that you do

let *v* to say that someone can have or do something

meal *n* something that you eat at a certain time of day; breakfast, lunch, and dinner are meals

Unit 6

lawyer *n* someone who learned the law and who helps people

job *n* the work that you do for money

sell *v* to give something to someone who pays you for it

follow *v* to do what something or someone says you should do

heart *n* your feelings

ride *v* to sit on something like a bike or a horse and make it move

way *n* how far it is from one place to another

by oneself *adv* without another person

tent *n* something you sleep in outside; you use cloth to make a tent

clothes *n* things that you wear, like pants, shirts, and coats

funny *adj* someone or something that is funny makes you laugh

perform *v* to be in a play, a concert, a circus, etc.; actors perform

adult *n* someone who is older than a teenager

Unit 7

hang *v* to fall freely

straight *adj* with no curve or bend

kind *adj* nice and good to people

art *n* beautiful things like paintings, photographs, or plays

anywhere *adv* to any place

use *v* to do a job with something

keep *v* to make something stay the same

dry *v* to stop being wet

cut *v* to make something shorter

side *n* the right or left part of something

purple *adj* with a color between red and blue

problem *n* something that makes you worried

windy *adj* with a lot of air that moves

flat *adj* not high

Unit 8

bird *n* an animal with feathers and wings

own *adj* a word that you use to say that something belongs to a person

jump *v* to move quickly off the ground; you use your legs to push you up

catch *v* to find and keep something

wind *n* air that moves

above *prep* over something

just *adv* no more than

person *n* a man or woman

engine *n* a machine that makes something move

business *n* a place where people sell or make things

popular *adj* when something is popular, many people like it

sport *n* a game that you play to have fun

Unit 9

inside *prep* in something

glass *n* something that you can see through; there is glass in windows

only *adv* no more than; just

alone *adv* without another person

newspaper *n* papers with news on them; many people read the newspaper every day

refrigerator *n* a big box that keeps food cold

climb *v* to go up or down; you use legs and/or your hands

floor *n* the part of a room that you walk on

tourist *n* a person who visits a place away from home

artist *n* a person who makes or performs art

food *n* people and animals eat food to live

egg *n* a round thing from a bird that people eat

other *det* a word that you use to talk about people or things that are different from the ones you already said

Unit 10

high *adj* far up from the ground

floor *n* all the rooms at the same level in a building

reach *v* to try to touch something

plant *n* something that grows from the ground, like a tree or a flower

lucky *adj* something that is lucky brings good things

also *adv* too

strong *adj* when something is strong, you cannot break it easily; powerful

earthquake *n* a sudden moving of the ground

damage *v* to break something

elevator *n* a machine that moves people up and down in a tall building

modern *adj* very new; not old

by *prep* not later than

Unit 11

cook *v* to make food hot and ready to eat

kitchen *n* a room where you make food

way *n* how you do something

on top of *prep* on the highest part of something

fish *n* an animal that lives in water and swims

short *adj* not long

strange *adj* very unusual or surprising

agree *v* to think the same as another person

so *adv* a word that makes another word stronger

taste *v* to give a certain feeling when you put it in your mouth

smell *v* to notice something with your nose

gas *n* something that you put in a car to make the engine work

save *v* to not use so much of something, like time or money

Unit 12

give away *v* to give something to someone without getting money

decide *v* to choose something after thinking

gift *n* something that you give to or get from someone

difficult *adj* not easy

save *v* to take someone away from something bad

win *v* to be the first or the best in something you play, like a game or the lottery

buy *v* to give money to get something

truck *n* something like a big car that can carry many big things

school *n* a place where you go to learn

winner *n* a person who wins

explain *v* to tell someone about something to help the person understand it

Unit 13

wolf *n* a dangerous animal that looks like a big dog

study *v* to use your time to learn about something

wild *adj* when something is wild, it did not grow or live near people before

during *prep* while another thing is happening

lesson *n* a time when you learn something with a teacher

music *n* the sound that you make by singing or playing an instrument

zoo *n* a park where wild animals live and people can see them

clean *adj* not dirty

fruit *n* apples, bananas, oranges, etc., are fruit

leaf *n* one of the flat green parts that grow on a tree or other plant

careless *adj* when you are careless, you do not think about what you are doing

responsible *adj* a responsible person is someone who does the right thing

Unit 14

go around *v* to go in a circle

wild *adj* exciting; not calm

ride *n* a trip in a car, train, bike, etc.

confused *adj* when you are confused, you cannot think well

really *adv* very

ever *adv* at any time

seat *n* something that you sit on

a few *det* some, but not many

toilet *n* a big bowl with a seat usually in a bathroom

rest *n* the time when you are quiet or sleeping

the rest *n* what is still there after you use some

Unit 15

each *det* every

holiday *n* a special day when schools, banks, and some businesses do not open; New Year's Day is a holiday

find out *v* to learn something that you did not know before

enter *v* to give your name to someone because you want to be in something like a contest

thin *adj* not fat

as...as *conj* words that you use to compare two things

pencil *n* a thin piece of wood that you use for writing

than *conj* a word that you use to compare two things to show how they are different

never mind *interj* no problem; it doesn't matter

dance *v* to move your body, usually to music

a little *adv* some, but not much

even *adv* a word that makes another word stronger

no one *pron* nobody

Unit 16

boat *n* a small ship for traveling on water

island *n* a piece of land with water all around it

row *v* to move a boat through water

race *n* a contest to see who can row, run, drive, etc., the fastest

scared *adj* afraid

go on *v* to continue; not stop

in danger *adv* in a bad situation

storm *n* very bad weather with strong winds and rain

wave *n* one of the lines of water that moves across the top of the sea

large *adj* big

lonely *adj* feeling bad because you are alone

enjoy *v* to like something very much

finally *adv* after a long time; in the end

be proud of *v* to be pleased about something that you or others do or did

Unit 17

build *v* to make something like a house or a building

stick *n* a long, thin piece of wood

stone *n* something very hard that is in or on the ground; a rock

heat *n* something that makes a place warm

light *n* something that helps people see in the dark

fish *v* to try to catch a fish

in a hurry *adj* when you are in a hurry, you must do something quickly

history *n* all the things that happened in the past

corner *n* a place far from the center

escape *v* to get free from someone or something

life *n* the way that you live

not...anything *pron* nothing

Unit 18

immediately *adv* very soon; in a short time

influential *adj* when you are influential, you can change people or things

become *v* to change and begin to be something different

star *n* a famous person, like a singer or actor

future *adj* happening at a time that will come

parent *n* mother or father

plan *n* something that you decide to do; the way you decide to do something

be against *v* to not agree with something

at last *adv* after a long time; finally

international *adj* between different countries

crowd *n* a lot of people together

Index

storm *n* 70

straight *adj* 30

strange *adj* 46, 49

stranger *n* 2, 5, 21, 33, 53

strong *adj* 42, 45, 73

study *v* 58, 61, 78

surprised *adj* 18, 21, 30, 49, 53, 65, 73

swim *v* 14, 73

T

take a bath *v* 14, 17, 38, 74, 77

taste *v* 46

teenager *n* 14, 17, 53, 58, 81

tent *n* 22

than *conj* 66, 69

the rest *n* 62

thin *adj* 66

together *adv* 6, 9, 37, 45

toilet *n* 62

tourist *n* 38, 45

traffic *n* 10, 13

travel *v* 18, 21, 22, 37, 42

trip *n* 6, 10, 18, 21, 46

truck *n* 50

U

unusual *adj* 6, 9, 18, 41, 49, 61

use *v* 30, 37

W

wall *n* 2, 38, 41

wash *v* 14, 58

wave *n* 70, 73

way *n* 22, 53

way *n* 46, 69

wet *adj* 14, 17, 49

while *conj* 10, 13, 62, 66

wild *adj* 58, 61

wild *adj* 62, 65

will *v* 10, 13, 17, 34, 42, 46, 50

win *v* 50, 66, 70, 78

wind *n* 34, 37, 42, 45, 73

windy *adj* 30

wing *n* 18, 34, 37, 41

winner *n* 50

wolf *n* 58

world *n* 18, 21, 42, 45, 58, 66, 74, 77, 78, 81

worried *adj* 6, 9, 45, 53

Z

zoo *n* 58

Irregular Verbs

Infinitive	Simple Past	Past Participle
be	was/were	been
become	became	become
begin	began	begun
break	broke	broken
bring	brought	brought
build	built	built
buy	bought	bought
can	could	been able
catch	caught	caught
come	came	come
cost	cost	cost
cut	cut	cut
do	did	done
drink	drank	drunk
drive	drove	driven
eat	ate	eaten
fall	fell	fallen
feel	felt	felt
fight	fought	fought
find	found	found
fly	flew	flown
forget	forgot	forgotten
get	got	gotten
give	gave	given
go	went	gone/been
grow	grew	grown
hang	hung	hung
have	had	had
hear	heard	heard
hit	hit	hit
hold	held	held
hurt	hurt	hurt
keep	kept	kept
know	knew	known
leave	left	left
let	let	let
lose	lost	lost
make	made	made
meet	met	met
must	had to	had to

Infinitive	Simple Past	Past Participle
pay	paid	paid
put	put	put
read	read	read
ride	rode	ridden
run	ran	run
say	said	said
see	saw	seen
sell	sold	sold
send	sent	sent
sing	sang	sung
sit	sat	sat
sleep	slept	slept
speak	spoke	spoken
stand	stood	stood
sting	stung	stung
swim	swam	swum
take	took	taken
teach	taught	taught
tell	told	told
think	thought	thought
throw	threw	thrown
understand	understood	understood
wear	wore	worn
win	won	won
write	wrote	written

Totally True 1

13 of 16

DATE	ISSUED TO

13 of 16

LINC